BLOODS AND CRIPS
The Genesis of a Genocide

Donovan Simmons
and Terry Moses

authorHOUSE®

AuthorHouse™
1663 Liberty Drive, Suite 200
Bloomington, IN 47403
www.authorhouse.com
Phone: 1-800-839-8640

This book is a work of non-fiction. Unless otherwise noted, the author and the publisher make no explicit guarantees as to the accuracy of the information contained in this book and in some

© 2009 Donovan Simmons. All rights reserved.

No part of this book may be reproduced, stored in a retrieval system, or transmitted by any means without the written permission of the author.

First published by AuthorHouse 2/11/2009

ISBN: 978-1-4389-3713-7 (sc)

Printed in the United States of America
Bloomington, Indiana

This book is printed on acid-free paper.

Dedication

I would like to thank my mother and grandmother, Mrs. Charlene Simmons and Mrs. Ressie Martin. Without you two I wouldn't be here. I love you both.

To my baby boy Tre'vion Simmons, I told you I was doing this all for you. You are my motivation to continue down a positive path. I love you and miss you.

To my Aunt Mrs. Minnie Martin, like I always say, no other aunt compares. I love you.

To my baby sister Tyresha Simmons, you need to stop being so stubborn. But I love you no matter what.

To my Uncle Jc, Joann, Louella, Nicole, and all my relatives: Zate, Nancy, Tange, Shine, Darwin, Bobby, Tameka, Carilee and her husband Brutie, and the whole Simmons family and descendants of (i.e, nephews and nieces), I send all of you my love.

And to the ones we have lost: Robert Simmons, Lapreece Simmons, Troy Simmons, Wess Wimberly, Sammy Wimberly, Victoria, Jw Bradford, Mama Annie, and Charles Hendrichs, we miss you and hold you dear to our hearts and you'll never be forgotten. We all love you.

Sincerely with love,
Donovan Simmons

Table of Contents

Acknowledgements ix

Introduction xi
   Poem – The Truth Is In Us xv

Chapter 1 – Death 3 Times 1
   Poem – Teardrops and Closed Caskets 7

Chapter 2 – Gang Violence Steals the Lives of the Innocent 9

Chapter 3 – Either Dead or in Jail 15
   Poem – Fallacy Fact 24

Chapter 4 – A Major Turning Point in a Destructive Era 25

Chapter 5 – Only 21 with a Bullet 29
   Poem – The Strength Inside of Yourself 34

Chapter 6 – Can't We All Just Get Along? 35

Chapter 7 – Just a Hyphen Between Two Dates 39
   Poem – Tales of Reality 47

Chapter 8 – Dead Man Walking 49

Chapter 9 – Aaren 57
   Poem – The Police Blues 60

Chapter 10 – Southeast Madness 61

Chapter 11 – Gangs' Destruction, Task Force Corruption 65
   Poem – Thought of a Broken Man 74

Chapter 12 – A Day in Life 75
   Poem – Hallucinating 82

Chapter 13 – Crack Cocaine, PCP, and Gangs 83

Chapter 14 – Haze 89
   Poem – Ghetto Love 94

Chapter 15 – Operation Safe Streets 95

Chapter 16 – War Stories 101
   Poem – War Story 109

Chapter 17 – Colors 111

Chapter 18 – Just Call Me Joe 115
   Poem – Because of You 120

Chapter 19 – Early Gang Devastation and Death 121

Chapter 20 – Stand Up to Adversity 127

Chapter 21 – Lost Love 135
   Poem – Shattered Thoughts of a Black Queen 142

Chapter 22 – What If 145

Epilogue 153

Appendix 157
   Poem – The Spirit and Legacy of Tupac 160

Introducing Calvin Offerral 163

Acknowledgements

First and foremost, I, Terry Moses, would like to thank co-author Donovan Simmons' mother, Charlene Simmons. You stayed through the rough with us, and without you this project would have never made it into print. Thank you.

To the following: Dr. Risely, D.O. and Jessie Snow (former librarian at Oakland Public Library), thank you for your words of wisdom and research.

To the Watts Library Branch, thank you for your vital research. WATTS UP!

To Sheila Faye, my sister Sandra, my son Terrell, and daughter Terriona, we are witnessing the true meaning of God's destiny as it showcases in our lives. I love you all.

From Donovan Simmons: I would like to acknowledge the following people. To L.P.T. Mrs. Block, Mrs. Rios, Mrs. Wooten, Mrs. Watkins, Mrs. Mohler, and Mrs. Carr, thank you for your words of encouragement.

To social worker Mrs. Laughlin and Mr. Brandman, PhD, thank you for keeping me focused.

To my Patna Victor "Boxer": good looking out on keeping it real.

Also, to Eddie Paradela, thank you for your help.

To Rona Johnson and the Lane family, thank you for allowing me to be a part of your family.

And to my editor, Susan Giffin, thank you for all your help.

Introduction

How many of us actually knew that when Crip founder Raymond Washington started the Crips it stood for Community Revolutionary Inner Party Services and the group was to represent black pride, black power, and was to focus on the major injustices that black people were going through at that time? The year was 1969, and by 1970 the Crips was a bona fide street gang with no intentions of fostering black pride or positive community services.

So now, almost forty years later, we are asking ourselves how did this happen at a time when the majority of the black teenagers wanted to be the next Huey Newton or Bobby Seales of the Black Panther party? I was a teenager at this time, and my name is Terry Moses. I helped start the Bounty Hunter gang, one of the gangs that fought against the Crips. From my personal point of view, I strongly believe a lot of things happened to turn us against one another. But I also believe that any one of us as individuals can only scratch the surface of the most devastating era of black-on-black crime in the history of the

City of Los Angeles and other cities that this virus affected, like San Diego.

So, I have hooked up with Donovan Simmons and other survivors from different eras to share their stories of how they survived, the losses, and the full effect it had on their families and friends. I think worth mentioning also is the fact that Raymond Washington was already in a neighborhood street gang called the Avenues. So it makes the definition of the word Crip very believable.

There is also a conspiracy theory attached to the history that I and others experienced firsthand involving the Los Angeles police and sheriff departments. You will be shocked and amazed at the part these professional law enforcement agencies played in fueling the flame of hatred.

A question that I have so often been asked is how did all the gangs that fought against the Crips become known as the Bloods? It happened when the Crips who, by 1972 was the biggest street gang in the city of Los Angeles, started to call anyone who was associated with the Crips by the word "Cuzz," which is slang for cousin. Before they started to use the word "Cuzz," we all called each other blood, which we all know as a word associated with black people as blood brothers due to slavery. As the years went by the word "Cuzz" became the signature word for the Crip gangs, while the gangs who fought against them continued to use the word "Blood," like other blacks did.

By the year 1976, to use the word "Blood" meant to the Crip gangs that you were affiliated with one of the gangs that they fought against, which resulted in non-affiliated people getting killed because they used a word that had been embedded in the black culture for hundreds of years.

By 1979, it was well known that anyone that used the word "Blood," affiliated or not, could lose their lives. So, it became a word that only the gangs used that fought against the Crips and that is how every gang that fought against the Crips became known as the Blood gangs.

This is a history that has left nothing but death behind it. But at the same time, it is a history that needs to be shared. I personally know ten people on California's death row at San Quentin State Prison waiting to be executed for gang affiliated murders.

Stanley "Tookie" Williams, who was the first popular original gang leader to be executed, lost his life in 2005. He changed his life while on death row writing several books denouncing gangbanging and giving the youth positive insight instead of a ticket to death row or an early grave.

And I think it is about time that we did the same because the truth of the devastating existence is in us and needs to be paid attention to. Like when I went to Juvenile Camp to serve a six-month sentence. The first letter I received from my "girlfriend" was telling me that one of my so-called homeboys was at her house trying to talk her up out of her panties. But as soon as I got out, I was willing to put my life right back on the line for this very same homeboy who didn't write me not one time. Something is wrong with that picture, but as gang members we become reacters instead of thinkers.

Our dedication to the gang won't or wouldn't allow us to see that the only thing in it is the loss of our own self respect, replaced by a false sense of homeboy love. Because that's what it was and still is. And some of the proof is in these prisons all over the United States. If you ask ninety-nine percent of the gang-affiliated inmates serving life sentences how many letters they have received from their homeboys in the gang that are still in the free world, the answer in just about in every case will be none. So, I advise the young to take heed to the true definition of the word homeboy. It means a person you know from home, where you grew up. Don't ever get it twisted with it meaning friend.

I also I don't believe for one minute that this book will bring a complete closure to the thousands of people who have suffered the loss of a loved one from this senseless kind of lifestyle. But what we do hope to gain from this is the attention of today's youth and show them that the color of a rag or the name of a street is not worth anyone losing their life for. So as I and the co-author Donovan Simmons narrate this project, we feel compelled to apologize for participating in something that became so tragic in the African American communities.

The Truth Is In Us

What's up, Blood?
What's up, Cuzz?
Was all that I heard,
and it's a fucking a shame
how what took place next came
from two funky ass words,
but now we say we're about our blackness
but that can't possibly be true,
because just for wearing the wrong color
your own will stab, shoot or
take full advantage of you.
Mothers crying over graves
cause their kids die before
they reach the tenth grade,
and for a black child to make it
past sixteen these days are mighty slim.
Bloods and Bloodettes,
Crips and Cripettes are caught up
in this cycle of madness,
and if our ancestors could see what we've become,
it would bring nothing but heartache and sadness.
Take big "Tookie," for example,
it took death row for him to realize
that he held so much beauty within himself
that hatred and violence wouldn't let him find,

but when he did, it almost
won him the Nobel Peace Prize.
Sure he caused a lot of terror on society,
but at least he tried to make amends
to create a different look, and I pray
to God that whoever has troubled kids,
they get the opportunity to read his books,
because the time has come for us
to quit hiding the truth and destroying
our youth and understanding should be
the beginning while representing
a color should be the ending.

Chapter 1

DEATH 3 TIMES

Name: Corvice Conner, a.k.a: Boco
Age: 42
City: Gardena
X Gang affiliation: Crip
Neighborhood: Shot Gun Crips

When did I start and how has it affected my life?

Basically this spiral began in the summer of 1978. I was in the process of going to the ninth grade. I was going to Henry Clay Jr. High. At the time, it was viewed as a bad school, and most parents in my neighborhood used false addresses to send their kids to a better school, like Peary Jr. High.

Actually Peary was a much better school. It was of mixed races and very strict. Even there, the Crips and Blood lingo (language) was involving. There were two emerging blood gangs going there—the One Hundred and Thirty-Fifth Street Piru Blood Gang and Centerview Piru

Bloods. The Crip gangs were Shot Gun Crips, the Payback Crips, and Twilight Zone Crips.

This was all new to us, because we were just kids. All we knew was we said Cuzz and they said Blood. And we weren't supposed to get along. So, on occasion we fought; girls even got involved. What I mostly recall is the togetherness this new activity brought on. It made you hang with those who rode your same bus. That's how it was determined where you were from. Whether you liked or not, you were grouped according to the bus you rode to school on. Therefore I, and most others, began to hang with my "home" boys and "home" girls. I recall feeling proud of my neighborhood.

At this particular school, we were outnumbered because this school was not our home school. It was a school which all of those from my neighborhood attended because our parents used false addresses to put us in a good school. So, our numbers were short and being so few, we really clung together. Ditching school, fighting, and misbehaving soon got me kicked out of Peary Jr. High.

This forced me to go to Henry Clay Jr. High, the very school my parents went through so much to keep me from going to. Henry Clay was actually as bad as thought to be. The faculty really didn't challenge you. You could ditch (skip school) and not worry about your parents being called. You could come and go by simply hopping the gate and return later or not even return at all. You could even fight and get away with it, simply by running away when the security guards finally came. So, I ripped and ran like everyone else, breaking into houses and then came the guns.

Just to have a gun was cool. The power of having a .22 or .25 in my waistband was exhilarating. I was intriqued with drive-by shootings. Not necessarily killing someone, but riding past a crowd yelling out my neighborhood and shooting two or three times. Hitting someone in the leg was cool enough to get you a reputation. Two or three or those drive-bys, and my rep was starting to grow.

We weren't automatically fighting against Blood gangs, but Crip gangs, too. I had a grudge against a neighborhood Crip gang right up the street from me called Ilium (one eleven) Street Neighborhood Crip Gang. I didn't like them. We fought against them at school, at local parties, and anywhere else we caught each other slipping (off guard). I had got caught slipping at a liquor store in their neighborhood by four of them. They blindsided me, hit me in the face, and I spun around instinctively and ran. Adrenaline gave me speed which was impossible for them to equal.

I ran back to my neighborhood park called Rowley Park, and told the homies the Ilium jumped me. We went and got our pistols, hopped on our beach cruisers, and made our way to enemy turf. My jaws was swollen and someone was going to pay. Foolishly, the same four who jumped me plus four or five others were hovering around their hangout spot, the liquor store on Imperial and Western, right across from Southwest College.

Excitedly, before we even got all the way there, we began shooting, scattering the crowd. I sure in hell felt good. It wasn't until later I learned we had shot two of them in the arm and leg, causing only minimal damage with the .25 automatic.

BEGINNING OF 1980

After getting kicked out of Gardena and Carson High, I was now going to Washington High, one of the worst schools in Los Angeles at that time. I was wild as can be, causing my mama to strive every which way and causing her to take off work each time to enroll me in another school or reinstate after a suspension.

In May of 1980, me and my homies (as we did every other weekend) took the bus downtown to the movies.

That was the thing to do back then, go to the show downtown and gather together with the homeboys at least ten deep, just in case of trouble. We would hop on the bus, mess with girls, talk shit, and hoo-ride (gangbang) on whoever we ran across, go see a Bruce Lee movie, and ride back doing the same thing.

Well, one Sunday we headed downtown. This particular weekend, the homie Lunchmeat was with us. He had gone to the Army and was back in the hood (neighborhood) on leave. I was happy to be with the big homie. Boy, was I acting a fool this day, talking shit to everyone, throwing rocks at cars, daring them to come back.

Well, on our way back we transferred buses on Century and Vanness; this was before they built the post on that corner. We're all on the bus stop, Lunchmeat, Big Bryon, Kenneth Price, and I, just to name a few, when this gold Cadillac rides by throwing up Inglewood family gang signs.

Shit, we went off. That's all we'd been waiting for was something to get into. We hollered back "Shot Gun Carip," while half of us ran out into the street to chase the car. Of course the driver timed this so as to make it through the light and keep going.

Approximately fifteen or twenty minutes later, as we'd now relaxed, one of the homies spotted the same gold Cadillac with the primer spot on the rear panel. Before anyone of us could react, a passenger leaned out the window and started shooting. We ran every which way, left, right or just laid down.

After all had settled, one homie was shot in the knee and the big homie Lunchmeat lay bleeding from what looked like the ear. As we all lifted him up, he was dead, shot in the back of the head by his ear. We were in shock. In fact the whole hood was stunned. This was our first gang death. I'll never forget the sadness the entire hood felt.

We all hung out at the park, mapping our response. The homie was dead. Only to be worsened by the fact he had entered the Army to change his life, came back on leave, only to be killed. Homies who didn't gangbang were willing to retaliate. This killing, our first, was like an assault on the entire hood, and everyone loved Lunchmeat.

We went back in groups to bust back (shoot back). The homie Mad Bill led the way, using his white van. Night after night, he led a crew to Inglewood, shooting anyone who looked like a banger. If they had a perm in their hair or wore red, they were getting shot. Back then the Inglewood Family Blood Gang wore perms in their hair. They had a certain look.

By now I was itching to get involved in the action. Hearing the stories the next morning of how the homies "got off" (shot a gun), not only did it make me proud, but also envious because I didn't have a story to tell.

One morning, while I was still at Washington High, I ditched school to burglarize a house. The purpose was to come up on some guns. While in the house, I stumbled upon a set of keys and by chance went to the garage where I found a Lincoln (car). The keys fit; I couldn't believe it, my very own "G" ride (stolen car). Inglewood here I come.

My homie T.J. (a.k.a. Crazy Troy) ditched with his girl Sweet Chocolate. She also went to school in Inglewood, and knew the Bloods by face. I picked them up, we got our gun, a .38 special, and Sweet Chocolate led the way to Inglewood High where we found them kicking it on lunch break. We circled the block, switching drivers, with me now in the shooter's seat (passenger's seat). We came back by, and I leaned out the window and shouted "SHOTGUN FOOL!" shooting five times. We drove off slow, cheering, happy, and feeling good, not knowing if we'd done any damage.

A security guard with Hawthorne police later stopped and arrested us. As youths we went to the California Youth Authority, we really didn't care. The bigger picture was we got off for the homie and for the hood and committed the boldest act yet, shooting at Inglewood High.

I did two-and-a-half years in CYA for that. I got out in December 1982, full fledged with a reputation under my belt. I did time for the hood.

Later in the eighties, I was in and out of the Crip Module 4800 located in the Los Angeles County Jail. It was one big cage full of chaos where they kept all the Crips at. The Blood gangs were also caged up the same way, separated from the general population. If you were or your hood was weak you would be jumped on, if not sexually molested.

All this was school, making me the hardened criminal I was becoming. Everything was about reputation. It was everything. It was not just about respect from your own hood, it was about making the enemy respect you or fear your name. But with that came consequences. Not only did the police target you, but also the very enemies you aimed to make fear you, target you, too, to enhance their own reputation. A never-ending cycle of unjustified madness.

And for the young people, I advise you to not believe the hype because the future for you as a gang member is death, death, and death. To you, if you get caught slipping, to someone you know or a loved one, and death row for the never-ending cycle of revenge, death three times and remember while you're wasting your time, another life will be hard to find.

Teardrops and Closed Caskets

A body drops, not a sound or word is heard.
The homie lay dead from a blow to the head.
This all happened all over words someone said.
It's a shame that a word or hand gesture will
have another seeking the fame
to end a another's life.
But on that day that's all it took
for the homie to lose his life.
Now a mother mourns a son she once bore,
Leaving her with the question why her son
had to die. When would this senselessness end,
she tries to comprehend,
while standing by his grave spilling tears
she knows she'll shed for years.
The homies tell her,
her pain won't be in vain,
an eye for an eye,
someone else must die.
As she looks into the future
with no justification of why;
and all she could see is another mother cry.

Chapter 2

Gang Violence Steals the Lives of the Innocent

"Look out," somebody screamed as a car drove by and just started shooting at anyone that was out and about. When the gunfire ceased, my brother-in-law Sherman Dobbins was shot, laid out, shot by a drive-by shooter. The Nickerson Garden Projects was where this took place at. Sherman was a married man in his forties that had nothing to do with gangs. The location, which was the projects, was the target because this is where the Bounty Hunter Gang resided. Rival gangs always came through with the intentions of killing a Bounty Hunter Gang member but usually end up killing someone who was just concerned about taking care of his or her family, as my brother-in-law Sherman. He died in the hospital a few days later from the gunshot wounds he suffered.

This kind of thing happened all over Los Angeles where innocent people took a bullet that was intended for a gang member just because they lived in a neighborhood where a gang was located. The stupid part of this is when gang members attack any place like a project, they are under the false assumption that everybody from this certain hood is affiliated with that gang and start killing up innocent people. Old ladies, little kids, it didn't matter; we've seen it all. Every gang is guilty of stealing the lives of innocent people. My sister Boobie Dobbins lost her husband because she lived in the projects. Rage always follows these senseless killings but no matter how many times there is a retaliation, that innocent person is still dead.

These horrific events weren't taking place just in Los Angeles; they occurred any place where there was gang banging. South of L.A., in San Diego, California, was no exception.

On a June night in 1995, an innocent life was taken by gunfire. What happened was an honor student by the name of Willie Jones was gunned down at a party in the neighborhood he grew up in. Unfortunately the community that Willie Jones was raised in was gang infested, so, there were a lot gang members at the party. An altercation occurred between the gang members; someone was slapped and kicked out of the party. Later after the party was winding down, a car pulled up in front and guys started shooting, killing Willie Jones.

This senseless killing devastated the community. Willie Jones was so liked by his neighbors that they filed a petition to change the name of the street he lived on to Willie Jones Street, which is what it reads today.

A metaphor of *de ja vu* is what I feel from the similarities of this continuing madness. Ten years earlier in Los Angeles, at Locke High School the life of an A student, track star, and brother of Olympic gold medalist Valerie Brisco Hooks, lost his life. Valerie had just won four gold medals in the 1984 Olympics, so, her younger brother had to have been highly motivated by the success of his big sister.

Bloods and Crips The Genesis of a Genocide

One day in 1985, he was working out on the track which is attached to the football field. It has a open view to anyone walking or driving by. Now, at this time Locke High had so many different gangs there that the school was a melting pot for gang violence. Young Hooks was doing his daily workout, sprinting around the track, when a car pulled up and commenced to fire shots at him. The rounds found their target and another innocent kid's life was stolen away from him and his family. Like Willie Jones getting a street named after him, the Locke Field was named Hooks Field in honor of the young man's life, de ja vu.

It needs to be said that in the areas that had nothing to do with gangs, this is why so many innocent people have been killed. The unaffiliated paid the same consequences as the affiliated as long as the neighborhood was the same. It's like paying an extra price for living in the inner city, because at the time you're doing your best, before you could pull your life together and move on, you lose your wife, son, daughter, mother, father, sister, brother, or even your grandmother to gang violence.

I personally feel like I have a moral duty to keep the memories of these people alive. And my family, as well, has suffered tragic loses. As mentioned, my brother-in-law Sherman was gunned down and he was also an innocent bystander. In 1994, one of me great nieces named Sonia was shot in the back with a AK-47 assault rifle. She was sitting at the dinner table when the shooting broke out nearby outside. A bullet came through the wall of the house then went through the back of the chair entering her back. And this was a shoot-out going on she knew not a damn thing about, but she became the victim.

She survived but that's not the point. It's the fact that another innocent person fell victim that had nothing to do with the senseless madness that was taking place outside of her house. It's a small world, and you never know when you're going to run into someone that you or your gang has affected in a tragic way.

In the year 1976, I was fresh out of the California Youth Authority, YTS also known as the Youth Training School. A few road dogs (partners) and I started selling heroin and PCP, but we were still doing the gang thing too. One night we sent J.T. a.k.a. Johnny Thomas to the all-night eating place called Stops to get us some burgers. Now, Stops set right across the street from the Nickerson Garden Projects which is where we were at. But J.T. took like two hours to come back with the food.

When he finally returned, we asked him what took him so long. He began telling us about this female he met that was stranded at the fast food joint. He said that he drove her all the way to Long Beach, which is a nice ride from Watts, considering you got people waiting on you to bring them some food.

The female's name was Red and she was one good-looking girl. J.T. was introduced to her sister Tee, also. They thanked him for making sure Red got home safe and gave him a number to call them so he could contact them later and get together and do some partying or just socialize. When he shared this news with us we were all smiles. We set a date up for that weekend to go out to Long Beach to enjoy ourselves with the ladies.

Once out there, we all coupled up and started to get to know each other. The first few times we just stayed in the Long Beach area. But once they got comfortable being around us we started taking them to different places. We all had ladies in the projects so we definitely could not take them to the projects, because project females have a understanding of zero when it comes to their men. So, we took them to different places around L.A., avoiding the projects.

One of my friends named Neal had his mother's garage hooked up liked a apartment. So, we took them there one evening to just sit around with drinks and food and to enjoy each other's company. Neal had his photo books laid out so they could look at some of the flicks. Red's sister Tee was looking through one of the books, when she screamed real loud, "That's him! That's him!" and then she dropped the photo book and started crying.

We all were in shock, but didn't have a clue to what she was upset about. When the other girls finally got her to calm down, she picked the photo book back up and showed us a picture of one of our home-boys and said "That's the mother-fucker who killed my baby."

We all looked at each other, and the incident immediately flashed in our minds. It happened in 1974, while she was coming out of a store when shooting broke out. Her baby was struck by a bullet and killed instantly.

It happened to be one of our homeboys who was convicted for this. He received thirty years but after ten years the case was over turned. It just don't get any worse than that.

There was just nothing that could be said to make her feel any better, so we all departed in silence. We never saw them again, but I would ask people from Long Beach who knew them how were they doing. Another life stolen by gang violence leaving a mother devastated beyond description.

The violence depicted here is only a very small percentage of the lives that were taken senselessly and too soon due to a way of life that should have never even existed.

Chapter 3

Either Dead or in Jail

Gangbanging. Crip and Blood. Those two words are the most devastating words ever spoken in or represented in my era. Those two words have split up families, put brother against brother, cousin against relative, and believe it or not, father against son. They also have left so many grieving mothers with the question why? And for me personally, I have lost so many friends to them two funky ass words.

I would now like to ask for your undivided attention for just a moment. Allow me to properly introduce myself. My name is Donovan Simmons, a.k.a Nitti. And my story begins south of Los Angeles in the city of San Diego (Southeast District). I have been affiliated with the words Crip and Blood and, more so, Piru since the age of ten.

The first incident I can recall involving those two words happened in 1987. I was over a friend's house one afternoon playing some Nintendo when some of his conrads that I was familiar with came over. I knew they were affiliated with the Crip gang, which was cool with me because I grew up with these dudes. But was I ever wrong. One of them by the name of Dre step'd to me and said "I heard you've been hanging around with Bloods."

Before I had a chance to reply, I was blindsided by a hail of punches. I managed to make a break for it and run home where I grabbed my father's gun and went back and shot Dre.

This was my beginning with those two funky ass words. But it doesn't end there. Like I said previously, I have lost so many friends living this way of life. I remember the homie who died in 1984. His name was Ricky Sykes a.k.a little Goddie (Skyline Piru). He was brutally beaten to death by rival gang members and left by the railroad tracks. His death has made a major impact on the Bloods and Crips in Southeast San Diego. Till this day, every gang member (Blood or Crip) throws up their gang sign. in memory every time they go over the railroad tracks, because the tracks go through the cemetery.

Even though I was only ten at the time of Mr. Skyes' death, the chaos that ensued was felt by all ages. A war between the Skyline Piru Blood Gang and the West Coast 30s Crip Gang was at full force. There were casualties on both sides and some the innocent was caught in the collateral damage. It's painful anytime we lose a love one, whether it's from gunfire or natural causes. The pain's the same. All the senseless killings over a word or a color, when you add it all up it doesn't compute.

Like I said, I was young when Mr. Sykes passed, but I have many close friends who I grew up with who met the same fate. Like my homeboys William Mathis, a.k.a Ck bill (Skyline Piru Blood Gang). There's so much I can say concerning this individual. I have known him from grammar school to the Boy's and Girl's Club to Juvenile Hall, California Youth Authority, and the penitentiary. He was one of a-kind. It's sad that his life had to end at the age of 24. He

Bloods and Crips The Genesis of a Genocide

was found dead with multiple gunshot wounds beside his car in the wee hours in April, 1998.

My father had a saying, and that was "You would be dead or in jail before the age of 25." I guess you can say he was psychic because in my case and a lot of my friends' cases, this came true.

I remember my first time in the California Youth Authority (CYA). Those of you who have never been or doesn't know anyone who has probably can't relate to what I'm about to say. CYA is a world within itself. It breeds and feeds off of violence. I have seen dudes come in who were weak or, as the saying goes, soft as cotton. But when they left they were monsters. That's what CYA will do. It will turn the weakest into the strongest and the strongest into the weakest. It's a constant ongoing battlefield. To have experienced both the penitentiary and the youth authority, I'd choose the penitentiary any day.

I remember a weekend when my family was coming up to see me when I got into a altercation with another dude. His name was Horse, and he thought he was big shit. I was on the phone calling to see what was taking my family so long and also to see was everything alright. They were driving from San Diego to where I was at in Stockton. That's a nine-hour drive.

Anyway, Horse was mopping the floor in front of me when he mopped over my foot. I asked him to apologize. He replied "Fuck you." I said, "The same to you." The next thing I knew he had hit me with the mop ringer, and we started fighting. While we were fighting, I heard my name being called for a visit but that didn't stop me. What stopped us was when the officers ran into the building and started macing and beating us with their nightsticks.

Only when I was lying on the floor did it registered that my family drove all that way and now they would not be able to see me. But luck was on my side because my counselor came and got me and told me to go to my visit; this would be taken care of later.

From the second I stepped into SRCC (Southern Reception Center of Correction) to the minute I left CYA, I was fighting; it was non-stop. There was always something going on. The littlest thing would turn into a major event in a heartbeat. And I truly believe that the staff provoked a lot of the aggression that occurred.

For example, in SRCC, they had a violator building called Gibbs. The building has an "A" wing and a "B" wing. The Crips were placed on "A" wing, while the Bloods were the placed on "B" wing. When a person arrives at Gibbs, he is interviewed by the unit sergeant. This is to find out your gang affiliation so your could be properly housed. Well, there were times when the staff was looking for kicks or don't like a person on sight; they will house a Blood on "A" wing or a Crip on "B" wing. Believe it or not this happened a lot.

I was waiting to see the unit sergeant when a Crip (I can't recall his name) approached me and asked me where I was from. I guess he didn't like my response because the next thing I knew we were fighting. We were broken up by the officers and separated. I guess the officers were looking for kicks because I was placed on A wing with the Crips. My stay was short because as soon as I set foot in the cell I was fighting.

CYA is a crazy place. It's the stomping grounds for future criminals. There is no such thing as rehabilitation; don't be fooled. Those who've been can relate, because I know our story parallels. For those of you who can't relate, I tip my hat to you because this life is for no one. Especially for our youth. I can tell you I had homegirls who would have their kids dress in gang colors, throwing up gang signs, and have them talking in gang slang. The kids would be fresh out of diapers. It didn't matter though, because the homegirls thought it was cute. What's cute about a baby perpetrating a lifestyle that came to represent self hate and death? There's no future in that. And the kids are supposed to be our future, but what type of future can they have when they start off with both feet in the grave?

I remember when I was over this one girl's house. I was sitting on the couch when this little boy walked up to me and hit me in the leg and said "What's up, Blood?" I looked at him liked he was crazy. His mother started laughing, like it was nothing. Well, I am sorry to say that same little boy was murdered outside of a liquor store. His name was Keyon Price, and he was only thirteen years old. Another life wasted.

Reflecting back I remember seeing all the little kids running around the neighborhood. It never occurred to me that I was seeing the future bangers and killers. This brings to mind that saying the Crips had, and that is "We don't die; we multiply." In a sense that statement is true because when one dies, there is always another to take his place. It's just a senseless cycle.

I had a little relative named Sammy Wimberly, a.k.a. Sam Bam (may he rest in peace) who got caught up in this cycle. I remember when I got out of prison in 1996, he was the one who came and picked me up from the bus station. He had his little partner Frankie in the car with him. Mind you, before I went to prison, they were both little kids. All they were into were video games. But as soon as I opened the car door, I knew things weren't the same. They had Tupac playing at full blast with their seat tilted back. I know the mannerism and they had them down pat. From the sagging pants to the red flag hanging out of their right back pocket. This is how the Bloods represent and carry themselves.

The year 1996 was a wild year for me; that is, the little time I was out for it. I got out of prison in February, a few days after Tupac's CD "All Eyes On Me" came out. Almost everyone on the west coast was on a west coast trip. Tupac had everybody fired up. And just like Los Angeles, Southeast San Diego wasn't no different.

The Skyline Piru Gang was at war with everyone, especially the Lincoln Park Blood Gang, and I had to get out right in the midst of it. Me and Sammy became inseparable. Since he already had a crew, his crew became my crew. Majority of the people Sammy hung around with was from Skyline even though he was from the 59 Brim Blood Gang. But everybody respected Sammy because he was a down little dude.

I remember when we got into it with some Crips in the apartments we use to kick it at. It was the homie little Joe Bowdie (a.k.a. Speed) spot. He lived there with his girl and some more females. On this day they were throwing a barbecue. While the females was out back hooking up the meat, me and Speed were out front kicking it on the walkway. One of the female's baby's daddy shows up with his relative. Speed knew the dude frequently comes over to visit his baby's mama and her sister.

They approached us and asked did we wanted to smoke some weed. I told him I didn't smoke, but Speed said he'll take a joint. Both of them went into the apartment. Speed told me that dude was a Crip, but he was cool. We started chopping it up (talking) when Hollie (she was my girl at the time) called me into the apartment.

While I was talking to her I heard people arguing on the walkway. When I came back out to see what was going on, I saw Sammy (who had just arrived) arguing with the Crip. I immediately got between them. You have to understand that Sammy was only nineteen and slim, while the Crip is around thirty and big. Since I was fresh out of prison, I was big myself from lifting weights. So, I intervened and I tried at first to take Sammy down the steps to kill the situation.

But when we got to the bottom of the stairs, the Crip started coming down with his relative. As soon as he got to the bottom, it was on. I started fighting with the Crip while Sammy was fighting with his relative.

The next thing I knew, two more Crips came out of nowhere and jumped in. I don't know where Speed was at; all I know me and Sammy was in a mix match situation. The manager of the apartments came running out saying he had called the police and they were on the way. That got everybody's attention.

We all broke. I was on parole so I had to shake the spot. I jumped in my car while Sammy jumped in his. We met up at the spot we had in Skyline over the homegirls vanilla and Renika and another girl I was messing with named Ilee. Not too long after we got there, a gang of Skyline homies started popping up. They already knew what had happen, and they wanted to know what we wanted to do. I told everybody I needed to find out what happened to Speed. So, I called over to the apartments but I kept getting a busy signal. We all decided to go back over there.

We all got strapped up (guns) and jumped in our cars and made our way back. When we got there, I noticed Speed was gone. We set up shop on the side of the apartments. My pager went off. I recognized the number; it was coming from the apartments. I knew it was Hollie, so I called back. The first thing she said was they were gone and please don't do nothing stupid. I played it off and told her we're not about to do anything. I told her I'll get back at her and I hung up.

We saw the homie Little HB coming from the back of the apartments. He asked us what was going on. We put him up on what had happened. He told us the police were over there and the apartments were hot (being watched), so we better bounce. We all separated and went our separate ways.

21

I finally found out what had started it all. The word BLOOD. That's all it took to ruin the day and almost get someone hurt or killed. When Sammy came up the stairs, he had greeted Speed by saying "What's up, Blood?" What's that "B" like? The Crip (who was now on the walkway playing with his son) went off and started calling Sammy a slob (a derogatory word used by Crips to disrespect Bloods). And from there you know the rest.

I've experienced a lot of drama at these apartments. Like this one time me and Speed was coming back from a day of kicking it. When we walked through the door, we saw a light-skinned dude sitting on the couch. Unknown to me, this is one of the dudes from Lincoln Park Bloods on the Skyline hit list (name won't be disclosed).

Speed immediately got to trippin', because he knew who the dude was. He went to pull out his gun, but I grabbed him and told him this was not the time. So, the dude from Lincoln was given a pass. He and his girl hurried up and left.

A few days later we were all standing in front of the apartments when a car drove by with some dudes in it. They started throwing up the Lincoln Park Blood Gang sign, so we throw up ours. The next thing you know, we're in a shoot-out. We figure the Lincoln Park dude went back to his hood and told his homies where we be.

Yeah, a lot of drama; that's all gangbanging is. I remember all the dudes I used to kick it with in 1996, like Frank Nitti, Joe Pl, Donnie Ross, Little Bugs, Ck Bill, Little Lebobo, P Bo, and my little relative Sammy, all of whom died a violent death. And for the ones I don't know their whereabouts, like Pooh Nitti, Speed, Tega, Spookie, Little Ant, Marlly Marl, Boo, Cory, Sick L, and Little Cowboy. I say to all you, "If the gang life hasn't pulled you under, I pray that you wise up and recognize that gangbanging is a dead end. I know you heard this all before, but I must reiterate on it. This is soul food for those of you who are lost and starving.

Let's put this shit to an end. It's time for a change. And that change starts by changing one's mentality. As I look back on all the people who I used to look up to, I see the same mentality in all of them, and that mentality leads a person nowhere. All it does is make you neglect the ones who have genuine love for you, the ones who bear all the pain and burden when you end up in jail. And the ones who carry the pain when you meet an untimely death. Bottom line, it makes you selfish.

It took me along time to learn this and to see myself for who I am or for who I once was. Now, that I see, I can make amends. I hope the people who are living this lifestyle wise up, because your life can be cut short, either dead or in jail. And for all the mothers and fathers who have lost a loved one to this senseless way of life, I wish to express my sympathy to you.

And for my family, Tupac said it best "There's no way I can pay you back, but my plan is to show you that I understand you are appreciated."

Donovan Simmons and Terry Moses

Fallacy Fact

The gang myth, yea,
it was just like I pictured it,
with bullets constantly flying past my head
only to look up and find a innocent baby lying dead,
now everybody is screaming for revenge
so we end up doing the same stupid shit
our rivals just did,
because in this life it's an eye for an eye
but not one of us could vividly
tell you the reason why,
because we were trapped in a mythological lie,
taught to believe that we were each other enemy
only to find out later that you are really
biologically kin to me,
and when I finally did wake up from my stupidity
it was like my vocabulary didn't even belong to me,
I was speaking words like "berious"
instead of "serious,"
and when I went to apply for a job
the people thought I was confused and delirious,
so I left the place feeling kind of dumb,
realizing for the first time that being raised
by the gang was not at all fun,
and the myth that ultimately became reality,
well it filled my life with nothing
but heartaches and tragedies.

Chapter 4

A Major Turning Point in a Destructive Era

Each and every time someone lost their life due to gang violence, a new killer was born. So many people had been killed by the beginning of the eighties that the name of the game was now revenge. The loyalty factor became so strong amongst the gangs that killing a rival gang member was more important than getting an education. By the mid-eighties, every inner city in all of southern California was riddled with Blood and Crip gangs.

The Los Angeles gang explosion spread from L.A. to San Diego when a well known L.A. Brim Gang member was gunned down by a rival Crip gang. The aftermath of this killing is still fresh on my mind. When Country was killed, the suffering was far from over with, because during his funeral that same rival gang rushed into the funeral parlor and shot the place up, and then flipped over the casket that his body was lying in.

This was the shit that people saw only in the movies, but we were living it and every day surviving it. This horrifying event took place in 1972 when the gang war was still young. Country's younger brother, who was called Little Country, was also a well known L.A. Brim Blood Gang member. His life was in constant danger after the killing of his brother, so he relocated to the City of San Diego, where a old gang was born in a new city.

The Five Nine Brims came to life soon after Little Country got there. This immediately turned into a gang war between the West Coast Crips of San Diego who started around 1974. None of us from the beginning of this senseless war knew that it would become what it did and the value of life would become so unvalued.

By the end of the eighties, the Blood and Crip gangs were in several states. This was mostly due to the crack epidemic that hit the inner cities in the early eighties. Crack cocaine became so plentiful and so many people were selling it; in order for some to make a profit they had to set up in other states. By setting up shop so to speak in other states, what also came with them were their gang affiliation. The influence of this was enormous. All you have to do is pay attention to what is taking place in Little Rock, Arkansas and you can see the Los Angeles Blood and Crip gangs reinterated only in a different place, but the results are absolutely the same—death at an early age.

By the end of the eighties, a lot of the original gang members were coming out of prison to find out that their kids that they had known no time for were now the next generation of gangbangers. And for some of us, our sons became fathers. So added to that, the type of lives that we were living, the results was a neglected child.

In the spring of 1988, I had just gotten out of prison. My stomping grounds were still the Nickerson Garden Projects even though at that point in my life I had been in prison twice. But my previous lifestyle had already dictated my future. So, I got right back into the gang life and drug trade. I was thirty-two years old, acting like I was sixteen.

One day soon after I got out, my son came over to the projects to see me. In the process of him and my nephew Big Harvey looking for me some young guys from the gang I helped start tried to jump my son because they said he was Crip. When they found me, I had no understanding after hearing this, and to my surprise while they were telling me what had happened the young guys were riding bikes not too far from where we were standing at. I called for them to come here which they did.

When they got within my arm's reach, I pulled out my pistol and commenced to pistol whipping each one I got close to. I never thought for one minute to ask questions; I just went into action because it was my son. Come to find out my son was a Crip, but by me not being a part of his life enough to know what was going on with him, I was totally blind. I had not grown out of that foolishness myself.

In me and my son's case, we love one another but this is what Donovan Simmons "Nitti" was speaking about when he said those two words, meaning Blood and Crip being so devastating in that era, that it was turning family against family. I was fortunate that those young gangbangers didn't come back later in the future and blow my brains out or jump me like I was the enemy like I had done to them.

This Blood and Crip thing, by the end of the eighties, was bigger than any of us. New leaders were taking over because of drug money. This turn of events turned Crips against Crips and Blood against Blood, while both still hated each other. Sadly the final results of this era can be found at your nearest gravesite and on death row at San Quentin State Prison, where I know fifteen people waiting to be executed for gang-related murders.

Like I said, this had gotten bigger than any of us, and more dangerous than any of us could have ever imagined, and if you were still alive you were still a target.

Chapter 5

Only 21 With a Bullet

Greeting, Dear Reader,

My name is Andrew Ervin a.k.a. Little Drew Loc. I am a twenty-one year old black male from San Fernando Valley, California. And yes, I too was a gang member; Crip, to be precise. I would like to dedicate my story to my generation in hopes they will acknowledge the futility in living this type of life. For those of you who took thirty years to figure this out, ask yourself this question (I know you already have) what if I knew what I know now? I know I am lacking the age experience, but what's the difference between dodging bullets at age thirty or age twenty? I don't see the difference. So, please weigh what I have to say and then and only then make your judgment.

I was initiated into the Crip gang at age ten. I guess you can say I was a spiteful youngster because the people who I chose to associate with were not my father's cup of tea. My father used to tell me over and over again to stay away from those boys on the corner. He couldn't understand the fact that whatever he said, I was going to do the opposite.

I wasn't out to make my father proud. In many ways I was out to hurt him. And it's safe to say I accomplished my goal in doing just that, because I have been placed in one foster home to the next.

This is how it unfolds when you choose a gang over family. You hurt the ones who have unconditional love for you, for those who have no love.

I hear it all the time, "That's my homie." I can't understand how you can call a person your friend or homie, when he stays tempting you against your family. Those are the type of people I chose to surround myself with. This was my banging crew. The Mighty O.V.G. Crip Gang, the ones who I thought had all the love in the world for me.

We had a place where we all hung out at. It was called the Dam's. This was where we plotted all our expeditions. This was also the place where you were initiated. Now, for you to be initiated into our gang you had to suffer a beatdown and go on a mission. It's a whole different story for girls. They have to have sex with all the homies, basically be gang raped. I have seen it all in the Dam's. From gang rapes to murder. To be in the gang life this was the place to be.

I had a friend named C-note. Now, C-note was crazy in every sense of the word. He loved to go on missions. He also loved to create missions. For those of you who are not familiar with the term mission, a mission is anything from a theft to a murder. And for C-note he loved the latter.

I remember one night when C-note and I were coming from some girl's house on the other side of town, we had to go through enemy territory called Huffy Park. While walking through the park, C-note pulled out his gun and started shooting. We ran all the way back to the Dam's.

Now, I didn't see nobody and I told C-note this, and you know what he said? He said he didn't see nobody either, he was just shooting in hopes someone would come out so he could have someone to shoot at. This is how it was with C-note. You never knew what he was going to do. I don't know what happened to C-note because I was moved to a foster home.

I have been bounced from one foster home to another, and in every home the family thought they could change me. You can't change someone who doesn't want to be changed. Things got worse for me, because I started following in my biological mother's footsteps by doing drugs. For her it was cocaine, for me it was sherman (PCP). And just like my mother, who I haven't seen since birth, it landed me in jail (Juvenile Hall). They call the Juvenile Hall system "Gangbang Central."

My first time, I only stayed two days, but during those two days I got into fight after fight. I was jumped too many times to count, but I was having a ball. This was the life.

When I was released, I was placed in a foster home in Fontana; and just like my previous family they thought a change was going to come. My foster father sat me down to lay down the law—no gangbanging, no drugs, and in the house before 9:00 P.M.

The first night, I broke all of them and then some. I was spinning out of control. I had a older friend who had been living this lifestyle all his life. He tried to enlighten me to change before I ended up dead or like him. He didn't understand; I wanted to end up just like him. I had pastors from churches tell me to give up this way of life. Did I listen though? Hell, no! My life was to the gang, and I didn't want to hear nothing else unless it had to do with Crip. That was my God.

I didn't have an ear for what they had to say until my God turned on me. I remember when it all started. I just got out of the California Youth Authority and I was homeless. I met up with one of my friends and I told him I needed somewhere to stay. I couldn't stay with him because his girl wasn't having it. So, we found an abandoned house.

He told me he'd be back to kick it with me; I haven't seen him since.

I left and went to Moreno Valley where a lot of my comrades were. I finally found a place to stay with a homeboy. He had a girl who had a cousin and man, was she fine! She could of been a model. His girl hooked me up with her. And from the first day it was me and her against the world. Everything was going all right until I started smoking sherman again.

One night when I was in one of my sherm intoxicated hazes, I saw a car with a red bandana in it. I set the car on fire. Little did I know, a police car was at the corner. Here I go again, back to jail, the real jail, no more Juvenile Hall. The first night I'm there, my so-called friends are trying to hook up with my girl. I told my cell mate what was going on. He is what we call an O.G. (original gangster).

After I told him, he started laughing. He said "You didn't know? You don't have any real friends in this game. Those dudes don't care about you." He told me I better wise up and realize I'm on my own. Later that night I thought about what he said and for the first time in my life I understood. I was homeless and by myself. I got on my knees for the first time and asked God could he help me. I know I had put a lot of people in danger.

That night changed my life. I denounced gangbanging. I'm still incarcerated, but I have a new lease on life. I'm through with the nonsense. For all of you who want to gangbang, I'm letting you know you're playing the devil's game. The devil is the biggest pimp of them all; don't be fooled and end up a trick. Stop the nonsense.

And I'd like to once again mention that I am only twenty-one years of age. So, I want to thank my God for enlightening me at a young age because the road I was going down was leading me to nothing but an early death.

Thank you also for reading my story, and I pray that some other young guys get the opportunity to read this, so maybe they too will start to understand that there's a lot more to life than taking the life of someone else for the color of their shoestrings, or less.

The Strength Inside of Yourself

Keeping my faith and destroying my hate
is an unconditional fact to keep
my spiritual blessings intact,
because my faith is vital
to the state of my emotions.
It is dear to me like water is
to the fish that dwells in the ocean,
because there is a mental block
when you practice faith
but you are thinking hate.
It shuts off your positives and
locks your blessings behind a gate,
because hate is feeling that destroys
positives healing while faith
can restore bringing you love
and so much more, but it is a
personal journey that no one else can travel.
So, it is up to you to delete your hate and
enhance your faith if you want your blessing
to flow freely through that gate,
and personally speaking
my faith will be keeping
because I'll be no longer seeking,
but absolutely sure that the blessings
from my faith will forever endure.

Chapter 6

Can't We Just Get Along?

The year 1992 was a major breaking point involving the Blood and Crip gangs. It was the year that Rodney King took a vicious beating by the Los Angeles police. It was caught on video and the whole world got the opportunity to see how brutal these cops really were. It was something that we had been stressing for years, but to no avail. What made the Rodney King beating even worse was the fact that the cops involved were tried and acquitted. That means excused of all wrongdoing.

Well, that decision did not set to well with the people of Los Angeles, because a major riot broke out. The beating was one thing, but then when the jury acquitted the officers of any wrongdoing, that was a slap in the face of all people of color. The city went up in flames and people looted for almost a week straight.

Then Rodney King appeared on television speaking those now famous words of "Can't we all just get along?" What those words did was make the notorious gangs, the Bloods and Crips, realize that despite what they had previously been doing, which was killing each other, it didn't make much sense after seeing racism with wide-open eyes.

Some of the gangs' leaders got together with people like Jim Brown, Maxine Waters, and others who had been concerned and had watched these gangs kill one another for far too long. A gang truce was formed. This truce brought people together for the very first time, because a truce was tried in 1972, but failed and the killing had been going on non-stop ever since. Twenty straight years of killing came to a temporary stop because we all got a wake-up call that something bigger than all of us was still in full effect, but we had been so blinded by our hatred for each other that we couldn't see or understand that the real problems of racism, discrimination, and poverty had always been the real issue.

Obviously this truce did not last, but it did change some people's lives. Some woke up and never gangbanged again. What it reminds me of is people only come together when a tragedy happens. Well, it is a major tragedy just thinking about all the people I know personally that are on death row for a Blood or Crip gang-related killing. It's also a major tragedy to think about all the people who have lost their lives representing a color or a street that none of us can truly own.

It should not have taken a Rodney King beating for the gangs to understand that we were creating a genocide of our own people, and in some cases family. I say family, because there have been times when relatives have killed each other just because one was a Crip and the other was a Blood.

We need to wake up, people, and start paying attention to what's really important in this life. I personally can't think of anything more important than family. I also believe that if we start to learn more about ourselves and who we are, we will start to lose the fear of having to face reality, and eventually we will start to accomplish much more in life.

As once quoted by Nelson Mandela, the words of Marianne Williamson are so very strong in my life right now. She said our deepest fear is not that we are inadequate. Our deepest fear is that we are powerful beyond measure. It is our light, not our darkness, that most frightens us. We ask ourselves, who am I to be brilliant, gorgeous, talented, and fabulous? Actually who are we not to be such? Your playing small doesn't serve the world, there's nothing enlightened about shrinking so that other people won't feel insecure around you.

We are born to manifest that which is within us. It is in everyone. And as we let our own light shine, we unconsciously give other people permission to be the same. As we are liberated from our own fears our presence automatically liberates others. We must be able to conceive this in order for us to be able to believe it. So, it is vital that we pay attention to who we are because learning your full potential can take you mighty far.

Chapter 7

Just a Hyphen Between Two Dates

By Terry Hall

Growing up in Los Angeles, California as a young black in a gang was hell on Earth. Come take a journey with me as I reveal the aftermath of my travels. It all started on June 26, 1981 at Gardena Memorial Hospital. That is when and where I was born into the gang. My Dad and Mom blessed me in all red from the time I left the hospital identifying me as a baby born into the Blood gang. I have the pictures to prove this fact. Believe me, it was hard growing up with eleven brothers all from the same hood. It's like my future had already been chosen for me and I had no choice in the matter. My whole family, females and males are all from the Athens Park Blood Gang and have been since it started way before my time.

As a kid growing up, that's all I knew. It was in my bloodline, inbred deeper and deeper with everyday life. I fell in love with the gang and was committed "till death do us part." Having an entire family from the hood only made things a lot worse than they already were. It was like I had to put in more work for the gang than the other original homies kids that I grew up with did to get out of the shadows of my family, especially my Dad and uncle. They are very well respected members of the gang. I was always placed in their shadow, and I was never recognized for who I was and what I had done as a gang member.

I got tired of being a "chip off the old block." I wanted to build my own reputation, respect, and power. I wanted people to fear me when they mentioned my name, and for that I had to develop a new me. At the age of seven I learned how to use a gun. I shot a tree and even though the power of the blast knocked me down, it put a nice size hole in the tree, and it gave me the power I was looking for.

I became obsessed with guns by the time I was a teenager. I kept a gun everywhere I went and used them as much as I could because it made me feel like a man. One of my older homies saw that in me and sat me down one day and told me about Butch Cassidy and the Sundance Kid. I went home and told my dad, and he liked the idea of the name, but said it was too long, so my Uncle said, "How about Cass?" and I loved it and started to live up to it every chance I got.

I also started to notice everyone around me getting bigger and bigger in the gang. Not only were they beating up and shooting our enemies, but they were having big money selling rock cocaine. I was then taught how to distribute cocaine and get paid for it, at eleven years old. I started driving and got my own car. All the females liked me. I was having money, sex, and power. This was the life for me and nothing could ever change that.

I had a best friend who was in the gang with me. We did everything together. His name was Little Wood. Of course he was named after Clint Eastwood. We lived life and partied like there was not going to be a tomorrow.

We both vowed to be best friends and Athen Park Blood Gang members until we died, but only one of us kept that promise. I'll never forget that day because it changed my life forever.

It was the day that Little Wood got killed. I really started to see things different because a whole new side of me was brought out as I was grabbing him in his casket shaking him, telling him to wake up. I was only twelve years old and people only died in movies and the real reality of what I was involved in had not yet personally affected me until the death of my best friend. I didn't understand that I would never again be able to talk with him or walk with him. I cried because they had taken my soul from me and unleashed a beast. I held his sister and we both cried together as they laid his young body in the ground.

When I finally walked away from that gravesite, something in my heart changed. I wouldn't smile or eat. All I could think about was Little Wood and who could have done this. My best friend had been shot and killed and all I could think about was the pay back. I cared nothing about my own life anymore, because to me my life had been taken away with Little Wood. So, I went on a mission to hurt anyone that represented the color blue, gang-wise, because I was sure they were responsible. I started sleeping in trash bins and hiding under cars, up in trees, and even on roof tops. I went up to high schools and junior high school that the Crips went to, just to beat them up or shoot them.

I had to get revenge for Little Wood and at the same time I had built myself a very dangerous reputation. Everyone in Los Angeles, Compton, and Watts knew me. I had become something more than I had realized. To make things worse, my dad went to jail for a shooting and was facing life in prison. I was already brainwashed, so when the name Crip came up with being involved with my dad being arrested, it only put more fuel on the fire.

I was arrested myself for carrying a gun before I could cause myself and others more problems than I already was responsible for. I was fifteen at the time so they sent me to this juvenile hall called Los Padrenas. This is where I met other kids like myself, Blood gang members. We fought Crips together on a daily basis, and I loved it. I was there for one month, which seemed like the best month of my life. I was actually mad when it was time for me to go home. While there, I found out some other things about myself. I was considered pretty damn good at rapping and singing. I did this while being confined to the hole for fighting so much, but it was nothing I planned on pursuing because the bottom line was, I was a gang member from the Athens Park Blood Gang and that is what was the most important thing in my life.

And at that point in my life I had no intentions on changing. I went to high school at Centennial High, which has always been considered a Blood gang school. I liked learning, but I took everything I learned in school back to my hood to strengthen my reputation. I started watching Old Mafia movies, like "Scarface" and "Carlito's Way" and flicks like "New Jack City," "Menace to Society," and "Boys in the Hood." I also started to read military books about evil leaders, like Stalin and Hitler.

I then proceeded to mix all the things I learned with my street knowledge, and I became a complete terror in society. My Dad was gone, but I now had around fifteen of my younger homeboys following me. My cousins, uncles and most of my older homeboys were locked up like my Dad. I personally had no guidance because I wouldn't listen to my mother, and every time a homeboy got killed or beat-up I just got worse.

One of my uncles told me before he died to never leave a soldier behind and when our blood is in the streets, somebody has pay. I tried my best to live by that motto

Bloods and Crips The Genesis of a Genocide

because it was the way of my world. My uncle always had a way with words. He had been to the armed services and everybody called him Sergeant. He used to sleep with his eyes open, and when he talked his voice demanded attention. It's like now I carry him around in my soul. He would always say, "Life is just like a hyphen between two dates." I didn't know what it meant, but I knew for sure it meant something to me because it is my favorite of all the things he used to say. Life is strange and the longer you live the more you see and are suppose to learn.

After Sergeant died, I found out that my girlfriend of four years was pregnant and it was crazy because she was the sister of my best friend, Little Wood, who just passed away. I felt blessed because I was partly responsible for keeping the spirit of Little Wood alive. I loved my girlfriend, but not enough to stop gangbanging.

About three months into her pregnancy, I got arrested for a shooting and was sent to the Los Angeles County Jail to await the outcome. The first thing I was informed of was the color red or the color blue did not mean a damn thing because the blacks were at war with the Mexicans; South Siders is what they went by. It stood for Mexicans from southern California.

I never fought so much in my life, and it was not fun like when I was in Juvenile Hall. I signed a deal to go to prison. My girlfriend had a boy, and we named him Damu Wood. The name was a complete reflection of my dedication to my fallen homie and the Blood gang. It was amazing how my son looked so much like me, but sad to say I was on my way to prison.

I turned eighteen right around the time I made it to Tehachapi State Prison. And as tough as I thought I was, I was still scared to death entering prison for the first time. I remember walking into the prison and the first thing I heard was the correctional officer yelling at us. Then I noticed a sign that said "No warning shot is required."

I got over my initial fear and adapted to my new environment. I had a few fights with guys from other Blood gangs, not my rival Crip enemies. The first riot I experienced was nothing like the race riots in the Los Angeles County Jail. People were getting stabbed, gunshots were being fired. It was total chaos. I must have had an angel with me that day because I made it out of that without being injured. I ended up in the hole so I had a lot of time to spend alone and think. I came somewhat to my senses and was able to make parole.

I started singing and working out. I even enrolled in adult school, but I was still hanging out in the hood and since I had gotten out of prison I was being treated like a local celebrity. I started dressing my son in all red every day, just like my Dad had done to me.

One night after leaving night school, my girl told me my son was sick and we needed to go get him some medicine. While in the store, I was approached by this guy, he said, "What's up, Blood? You still banging Athens?"

I said, "Till my casket drops."

He replied by saying "That's right!"

Something didn't feel right, so I told my girl to take my son and get lost in the store. She started to cry, telling me please don't do anything, but I went outside anyway to see what was up. I found out as soon as I stepped out, because I was shot eight times by another Blood Gang member which was supposed to be my comrade in the war against the Crips.

I vowed that if I lived through this, it was now going to be a war against every Piru Blood Gang in the area. Obviously I survived and my new motto became, "Kill or Be Killed." For the next two years, I went on a gangbanging rampage. I was in and out of jail but I didn't care.

Me and my girlfriend had us another child during this time, a beautiful little girl. We named her Princess. There was something about her, because every time she smiled it melted me all over. I use to sing to my daughter and son. They loved it and it made me feel good.

People started encouraging me to sing, so I calmed down a bit and started going to the studio working on songs I had written, but all that came to an end the night they killed my brother. I tried my best to accept it and cage the animal inside of me. I had a flashback when I grabbed my daughter and son, my daughter started to cry and hold my real tight. That little girl had my soul, and I saw so much of me in her. I started to sing to her real loud, but she kept on crying like she knew what I was going through. When she held me real tight, I flashed back on when I was holding onto my best friend Little Wood while he was lying in the casket.

I saw the hurt in my daughter's eyes that she was feeling for me. I had her with me when I went to my brother's funeral and after that she was with me for the next two months straight. One morning, my daughter kissed me and said, "Bye, Daddy" and left the room. That was the last time I touched my baby.

I got arrested for several charges and was convicted. I'm in prison now for the next ten years, and I have not gotten one letter from my "so-called" homeboys in the gang. I now realize I wasn't a part of a gang, but a gang's puppet and when they couldn't use me anymore they snitched me out to the cops. Yes! That's right. The gang that I dedicated my life to and put before my kids, sold me out.

You see, that's what I now realize "a hyphen between two dates" means. Let me please clarify what I'm saying. When you look at a dead person's tombstone, it reads the name of the deceased and two dates, the one you were born and the one you died on. That's a hyphen that represents your life, so don't let yours stand for nothing.

I haven't talked to my son or daughter in a while, but my daughter visits me in my dreams and lets me know she's mad at me for leaving her. I've also learned to deal with my temper and I've started back writing music. I'm still changing from the person I was by learning to love myself first and foremost, then I can love and respect others as well.

And to all my fallen soldiers who never got the opportunity to change, rest in peace and no matter how many people tell you that gangs are what's happening, don't believe it, and if you do your education of a hyphen, it will be learned the hard way. So, my personal advice is to stay in school because it will be your education that takes you to great heights, not the gangs.

Tales of Reality

You are under the influence of the ghetto
when you have a hangover from hunger
and your stomach is growling like thunder
and when you wanted to go to school,
but you had no shoes,
so you're missing your education
because poverty and hunger
has taken reservations.

You are under the influence of the ghetto
when you become intoxicated on violence
and the rage you feel is no longer silent.

You are under the influence of the ghetto
when you sometimes wish that you were dead
or had never been born,
but your little sister is hungry
and holding on to your arm,
and when she looks into your eyes
the love you see cannot be denied,
so it is for her you know you must survive.

Chapter 8

Dead Man Walking

When I completed my research of the people on death row and particularly the African Americans, I was in a saddened state of mind, because I didn't realize until it was over that there were so many people condemned to death that I personally know. There are six hundred and sixty-eight people on death row in San Quentin State Prison. Two hundred and thirty-four of them are African American and one hundred and ninety-two of those people were convicted out of Los Angeles County.

After going over the entire list of the names of African Americans from Los Angeles, it was found that over one hundred of the one hundred and ninety-two were gang affiliated, being a Crip or Blood gang member. I feel compelled to mention these statistics because they are so vital to what has taken place over years concerning gangbanging. Some of these guys are literally going to die for a street gang that didn't give a damn about them. I also realized how these guys have been forgotten about after I got the opportunity to read a short testimony of condemned inmate Keith Fudge.

It has been over twenty years since I saw Keith Fudge a.k.a. Ace. I met him in 1985, when he was in the Los Angeles County Jail, facing seven counts of murder. It has now been twenty-two years, and these are the words spoken by Young Ace, as I used to call him back then.

From cyberspace.com: "Today I sit waiting in anticipation of my fate from the kidnapping, two decades ago, as a youth in the inner city of Los Angeles. In the clutches of the injustices. I struggle to prove my wrongful conviction as so many before me. I urge you to commit yourself to the truth and allow me to be free first in your mind and second in my life. I, the only child of a mother who awaits my return so diligently. Tears swell in her eyes as I absorb them in my pain of confinement.

"I have come to accept that my youth has been taken, however, I am not willing to accept that my life too will also be taken. I will fight and must fight to ensure that justice denied will no longer be a part of my life. With the strength I receive from God, Family and devoted friends I lift my eyes each morning believing in the faith that the truth will set me free."

That is just a portion of how Keith Fudge feels twenty years after he was arrested for the crimes he is condemned to die for. I personally believed him then and I believe him now. When he says he is wrongfully convicted, even though his case has been affirmed by the highest court in the country, he hopes to still, somehow, prove his innocence. Keith Fudge was a Blood gang member from the V.N.G. Gang.

When I met Johnaton George, who is now also on death row at San Quentin State Prison, he was fourteen years old. I was sixteen, and we were both in Fred C. Neles School for Boys, a California Youth Authority, in the year 1973. Johnaton was so huge with muscle mass at fourteen that he had to be housed with us older kids. And he still was bigger then us. He loved sports, especially football. We played together and against each other. And I must admit that it was a lot better having him on my team as opposed to playing against him.

Most of the people that knew him all thought that one day he would be playing a professional sport, but he could not stay out of trouble. Like me, he never stayed out long. Every time I went in the California Youth Authority, he was already there or on the way.

One night in the summer of 1996, I was at home watching the television. I had it on America's Most Wanted. When they showed Johnaton's picture on the screen, I told my girlfriend Jody that I knew that guy and had been knowing him since the early 1970s. They said he had just been caught for murder and it kind of made me think about what could have been for Johnaton.

He didn't hang out with the gangs, but he was affiliated with the Bloods because of an incident that happened at YTS (Youth Training School), another California Youth Authority. He got into a one-sided fight with a well known Crip gang member and ended up knocking the guy out with one punch. So, ever since then he was labeled a San Diego Blood gang member, but I can tell you from being around him he was not a gangbanger.

He had a brother who once played with the San Diego Padres professional baseball team. We all wanted to see this guy make it big in sports because we knew him and we were fully aware of his capabilities. Now he's on death row at San Quentin State Prison awaiting a response on his final appeal. And like me, he is probably saying, "Why didn't I listen to all the people who were trying to help me and guide me in the right direction?"

When most people think about a person on death row, the first thing that comes to mind is the crime that they have been convicted of. For me, it is a totally different emotion because I knew most of the people mentioned before they were convicted. Like my homeboy Mario Gray. I have known him and his family for more than thirty-five years. Mario was an original Bounty Hunter, but his sister Carrolyn was affiliated even before he was. She ran with the Bounty Hunter Gang from the beginning. Her brother Mario, who is now on death row for double murder, helped me out of a jam one day and we became close after that.

One day, back in 1972, I was at the liquor store that sits in our neighborhood, when this older guy walks up with his wallet in his hand. He looked kind of drunk so I thought I would take his wallet. I snatched it right out of his hand and proceeded to take the money out, then I was going to give him back his empty wallet. I did this all cool and calm because I knew I was not going to have a problem handling this guy if it came to that.

Well, before I could take the money out of his wallet I heard somebody say, "Look out!"

When I looked up from the wallet, a straight razor was coming for my neck. I jumped out of harm's way as fast as I could and missed the razor only by inches. I then went into action protecting myself because now he was coming at me, swinging the razor as fast as he could. I side-stepped him, then grabbed the old guy and tried to take the razor from him. Mario came over and took the razor out of his hand. We then broke together down the alley. I split the money with him because if it wasn't for Mario I would have gotten my throat cut.

As I got to know Mario over the years, I found out that he was very free-hearted with his money. I last saw him in 1987 at the Los Angeles County Jail, when he first got arrested for the crimes he is condemned to die for. We talked about old times, avoiding any conversation about what he

Bloods and Crips The Genesis of a Genocide

was in for. When we departed, I knew I wasn't going to see him again.

They came and took him to high power where they keep all the high profile cases. He has now been on death row since 1990, and his sentence has been confirmed by the highest courts. A life wasted that was heavily influenced by the unforgiving realities of street life.

The situation of being condemned to death for murder could have happened to anyone that is gang affiliated. Because you are considered a murderer by affiliation whether you pulled the trigger or not. Death row at San Quentin State Prison is full of gang members and ex-gang members from Los Angeles County. From the early 1980s to right now, I have watched guys I know get condemned to death. It's different when you look at the news and they announce that someone has been sentenced to death, you don't pay it very much attention, but when it's someone you know it's a whole different feeling. It's like that person's life flashes through your mind.

Like when I first heard that Regis Thomas was sentenced to the death penalty. The first thing that went through my mind was, "Damn! I've known Regis, better known as Reggie, ever since he was a kid growing up in the Nickerson Garden Projects. Me and his mother Iris are friends." Reggie was convicted of the killing of two Compton police officers back in 1992. His appeal is still in the high courts.

Dead man walking is the term that is used every time a death row inmate is escorted some place within the prison. It's a sound that you hear and immediately say to yourself, you're sure glad it's not me. The one thing that I express so strongly now when I speak to young people about the guys I personally know on death row is that it could happen to them, just as easily if they choose to continue to gangbang or start too, because they want to be associated with the tough crowd.

No one ever affiliated could look you in the face and tell you they got anything good out of gangbanging. It was a losing battle for all of us, but we were blinded by an unjustified hatred that we carried around for each other. I am not at liberty to say what I think the people on death row know and feel.

I can tell you how I feel and what I think needs to be done, so the next two generation won't meet that same fate as Stanley "Tookie" Williams did. He was executed by lethal injection at San Quentin State Prison in 2005. He was the first well known original gang leader from the Crips and Bloods era to die this way. I respected the work that "Tookie" did while on death row. He wrote numerous books denouncing gangs and tried to guide the youth that came in contact with his work in a positive direction. It was something he did not have to do. His fate was already sealed by his murder conviction.

The political sideshow they put on about "Tookie" not being executed was just that, a sideshow, to make the public believe they were considering not killing him. It was a very strong statement that was made to all death row inmates, because this man had been nominated for the Nobel Peace Prize for his work while on death row. So if they executed him who could have done more good alive than dead, that doesn't leave much hope for the others up there fighting for their lives.

My personal theory is we have to do our best to keep our lives from being placed in the hands of the executor. I also strongly believe that in order for us to get our message across to today's youth, the survivors of the beginning of this madness are going to have to participate. We have to take the initial steps in stopping it just as we started it. No mental health psychologist or juvenile delinquent counselor is going to even come close to bringing this to an end.

I feel like this is the most positive endeavor I have ever been apart of. And I get strongly motivated every time I think about the guys I know that are on death row at San Quentin State Prison. Big Time, Barry Williams, and Pee Wee are three other guys I personally know who are condemned to death row. We were dedicated to the gang, but the gang gave us nothing back in return. It passed us by like a strong wind when we needed help. It would not supply us with a twenty-two, twenty-nine, thirty-three, thirty-nine or forty-one cent stamp when we needed it so badly to write our families and express our regrets.

So many years have gone by and now the stamps are forty-two cents. It hurts me inside to think that not a person from the gang wrote me to even say good-bye. Dead man walking. Sometimes it makes me want to cry.

Chapter 9

Aaren

First, I would like to introduce myself. My name is Aaren. When I was gangbanging, they called me Dirty Left or BG Loc. I would like to start off by saying cripping and blooding isn't all what it's cracked up to be. Let me take that back; it is exactly what it's cracked up to be, because as I reflect, I realize I didn't get anything positive out of that way of life. All I did was create enemy after enemy. People who I've grown up with turned against me due to our representing opposite color flags. And for me, I had it harder due to being white representing a black gang. I've been stabbed, jumped, shot at, and shot.

People my age (which is twenty-five) think this shit is cool, but that's far from the truth. When a little kid can't go outside to play because his parents are afraid he'll catch a stray bullet from a rival gang, it's sad. I remember growing up playing football, baseball, and all that good shit. That's what I should of stuck with.

By the way my city is San Diego, and my gang was the West Coast 30s Crip Gang. I've been around this gang since I was nine years old, hanging around with the people I thought was the shit. I started hanging out then slowly but surely it turned into an everyday thing. When you make it to twenty-one years of age in the ghetto, you have accomplished a lot. Why? Well, I personally have been shot at by the police and shot at by rival gangs several times and feel fortunate to be alive today. I wasn't afraid to die because I thought my turf (gang) would praise and acknowledge me for the things I did while representing. I've stabbed and shot people, and for what? Because I thought these people were my loved ones, my gang, that is the so-called West Coast Crip Gang!

I was fighting for land and territory I didn't even own or could never own. I mean I fought hard and tried to kill people for looking at me wrong, even more for wearing red or a skinned head. The reason why I was stabbed was because I was a white boy from a black gang.

When I first went to prison it was the worse thing that could of have happened to me besides being dead. They got bullshit politics, race wars, and same race bullshit all the time. There is no more unity amongst the gangs, because there are times when your so-called homies will be the first ones to run on you when the drama starts. And me, well you would think that I would roll with whites; it didn't happen that way.

I was a Crip who rolled with Crips from San Diego. For that reason the skinheads came after me. I got jumped and got my ribs cracked. You would think I would have woke up at that point, but no I kept going back to prison and every time more shit happened to me. I got stabbed in the leg, got my head busted open, and a broken nose. I even got a eye ring snatched out from my eyebrow during a riot that broke out, which happened all the time in prison.

I can truly say that gangbanging has caused me more problems than anything else in my young life. Not only did

Bloods and Crips The Genesis of a Genocide

I hurt people but I made myself a lot of enemies in the process. I got stabbed in my other leg, got shot at and shot in the foot one time, not to mention being jumped more than a few times. So, living the life of a gangbanger, I had police enemies and rival gang enemies. The police shot me in the stomach then slammed me down on the pavement, and busted my chin open during the process. I know none of this sounds good, but it's the price and reality of living the life of a gangbanger. You also burn bridges with loved ones who you refuse to listen to.

I understand now that I was known in the streets for doing nothing but bad things and I got nothing but bad results, when I could have been getting an education. Then at this point in my life I could be in the position to be a mentor to a troubled youth. There are all kinds of positive things you can do to be loved other than gangbanging or selling drugs.

What finally stopped me from ruining my life was family. You can't raise kids in the streets, because if you do, then the streets will raise them and not you. You don't want your kids going through the same shit that you went through.

Well, I hope my story gave you some positive insight to do something with your life other than throw it away to the streets. And I hope this has inspired you to understand that family is the most important thing we have.

Thank you for letting me share my story with you. One love from Aaren.

Donovan Simmons and Terry Moses

The Police Blues

I've had the police blues for most of my entire life.
While some of the things I've saw and done
was nothing near nice, but it always seem the police
be trying to kill the same brother twice,
with a heavy dose of over kill
while your family is stuck
with the cost of the funeral bill,
but then they tell you to hold on
because there's going to be
an autopsy and investigation
while your love one has been sent
on a permanent vacation,
ten, twenty, or even thirty bullets in one body,
they'll still just say the officers were caught up
in the moment of action,
quickly to excuse that it was
really a case of racist satisfaction.
The police blues is the reality of the
hatred and brutality that I often saw,
which had nothing to do with the goddamn law,
and by some one dying every time
the police showed their face
seem to be a perfect place
for me to tell the jury, I rest my case.

Chapter 10

Southeast Madness

The madness that has plagued Southeast San Diego has gotten out of control. The gang epidemic has reached an all-time high. It pains me to see the city that I so much love affected with this virus. It's a tragedy. The gangs are uncalled for and they hold no real purpose. Unlike Los Angeles, where the gangs are spread out, Southeast gangs, on the other hand, are all in walking distance of each other. We all go to the same schools, same stores, and the same "Fam-Mart." We all grew up together and more then likely know one another, and in most cases are related.

Allow me to elaborate. You have the gang Skyline Piru Bloods connected to the Lincoln Park Bloods by the street Olivera. Lincoln Park is connected to the Neighborhood Crip Gang by the street 47. The Neighborhood Crips are connected to the Emerald Hills Blood Gang and Little Afrika Piru Blood Gang by the street Euclid. Also, the Neighborhood Crips are connected to the West Coast Crips by the street Market. The West Coast Crips are connected to the 59 Brims Blood Gang by the street Imperial. Everyone is connected, side by side. So, I have to ask "What's the point?"

Donovan Simmons and Terry Moses

If you was to ask one of the bangers today, why are they banging, why is the person down the street your enemy? They wouldn't be able to give you an intelligent answer. Prime example: Not too long ago I went OTC (out to court). If you didn't know, I am currently incarcerated. When I was in the county jail in San Diego, I had a cellmate from Skyline. His name was Poohbie. He was being accused of murdering a rival gang member. The gang rival happens to be from the gang Lincoln Park Bloods. These two gangs (Skyline and Lincoln) have been arch enemies since the early 1990s. Mind you, they're right down the street from one another.

I have been out of the loop of what's been going on in Southeast since 1996, due to being incarcerated, so everything that Poohbie was telling me was all new. It was a mind blower to hear how extreme, twisted, and powerful the hate has gotten. It's sickening. I had to ask him why? And you know what? He couldn't tell me why. All he said was "I just hate Lincoln." He didn't know why he hated them or how the war began. He just was involved and hated anyone representing the green flag. (Green is Lincoln color.) Now Poohbie is up against it.

It's just not him, though. A high percentage of the youth in Southeast San Diego is affected with this sickness. The cycle needs to be put to an end. I don't know all the answers for the solution. But I want to contribute all I can to find a solution, so the next generation won't fall victim to this senseless way of living. There are too many of our youth laying in Greenwood Cemetery.

So, to all you Southeast OGs (Originals)—Silk, Big Hollie, Pinky, Dannybobo, Double Troubles, Don Juan, Stace Soft, Art Louie, Federated, Baby Jack Nasty, B Bop, Craigo, Pringo, L.O., Tap, Finnie Boy, Top Cat, Crazy Cat, Big D, Con Man, Khaos, Big A, Shortcut, Red, Boo, Bull, Bob Cat, B hog, Ty Ru, Charlie Cat, Black Charlie, Charlie BoBo,

Mad Man, Bo Hump, Howie T, and Maddie Stone— Let's put an end to the madness and genocide. We're all family and we represent the same section of town, Southeast San Diego. It doesn't matter if you're incarcerated, your voice still can be heard and can make a impact in a youth's life. It's all up to us.

I remember hearing stories from the OGs, the ones who were around before the gangs, like Uncle Vino, Popa T, and Frank Nitti. They told me how all the blacks in Southeast used to meet up at Lincoln High and Oceanview Park on the weekends, when it was all about the cars and your attire, to be fresh dressed and represent yourself. Also, who can pull the fliest females. This is what it was all about. Black pride, holding your fist up. People forgot that the Black Panther Party was also in Southeast San Diego. So, Southeast hasn't always been a place of destruction for the Africans. On the contrary, it was a place where we as black people could be ourselves. That all changed with the gangs and drugs. It destroyed the black man and weakened the black family.

Like I said, it's time for a change and to get back to some of that Southeast love. It's all in us.

Chapter 11

Gang Destruction, Task Force Corruption

In the early 1970s, when the Blood and Crip gangs began to get out of control, the law enforcement agencies came out with their own notorious gang to combat the street gangs. The first of these was a task force called Team Twenty-Nine from the Los Angeles Police Department's Seventy-Seventh Street Division. Anyone that was active as a gang member got to know this task force up close and very personal.

In year 1972, Team Twenty-Nine made sure every gang in their district knew who they were. I personally got my ass kicked almost every time I came in contact with them. The Nickerson Garden Projects, which is where the Bounty Hunter Gang is from, already had a reputation of shooting at the police. They had been doing this even before the Bloods and Crips hit the scene. So, when Officer Edwards from the LAPD's Team Twenty-Nine Task Force got killed, the Bounty Hunter Gang caught hell from the task force. They hauled us in every day for questioning until they were convinced that our gang had nothing to do with the officer's death.

I had just been released from the California Youth Authority when the killing of Officer Edwards took place. One night, I was picked up off the streets by the police for nothing. While I was in the back of the police car, the two officers were talking to one another. The next thing you know I'm being booked for possession of pot. I'm in the back seat raising hell, telling them they were dirty for doing this to me. They knew I was on parole and they also knew by arresting me I'd be violated. Now, I've been to this particular police station before at least thirty times, but something was not right about the direction they chose to get there.

All of a sudden they pulled into a dark alley and turned off their lights. Now, I'm quiet as hell, because now I know some foul shit is about to go down. They talked for a minute or two, then one of the cops opened up the car door and literally snatched me out of the car. I was handcuffed so I hit the ground without being able to break my fall. The next thing I know I was grabbed by my neck and a pistol was placed to the side of my head. The next words I heard I thought would be the last words I would ever hear. The cop with the gun to my head said "This would be a good place to kill this nigger."

His partner then stepped closer and said to him, "Man, I told you we can't do it. I already dispatched it in that we were bringing him in."

I still hadn't said a word because I didn't want to piss this guy off while his partner was telling him he couldn't blow my brains out. The cop with the gun then kicked me a few times in my ribs, which I was thankful for, as opposed to being a statistic laying in an alley with half my head shot off.

Before these cops left me in the hands of the booking officer, they warned me with a threat on my life. The one that held the gun to my head told me I better not ever raise my hand to a Los Angeles police as long as I lived.

Unfortunately for me, I was arrested at the beginning of the year of 1975 for an assault with a deadly weapon on a housing authority police officer. The housing authority police were assigned to patrol the projects in the City of Los Angeles. By this time in my life, I was being blamed for anything that had to do with a shooting if I was not incarcerated when it happened.

Now, I'm in the backseat of the police car thinking about what those cops had told me they would do to me concerning the well being of their fellow officers. The housing authority cop had been shot with a shotgun in his face and body, but I was now hoping that when I got to the police station I wouldn't see the two cops who had threatened my life. I was hoping that they would put me in one of the cells that when the cops walk by they couldn't see you. Well, I wasn't that lucky. They put my ass right on display for all to see who were walking by. Two detectives came to the cell first.

They already knew me from my early juvenile deliquent days. When the cell door opened, I prepared myself to get the shit kicked out of me. But they just stood there looking at me, and then one of them said, "We're going to fry your black ass if that cop dies."

I tried to defend myself by saying it wasn't me. They shut the door while I was talking. I was still on CYA parole which stands for California Youth Authority. So, I couldn't bail out even if I had money, because a parole hold is placed on you when you get arrested while on parole.

Two days went by and I was still stuck at the station. They were supposed to take me to the Los Angeles County

Jail. I was thankful I hadn't seen those two officers that had threatened me.

On the third day something happened that only happens once in a lifetime. The jailer came to my cell and said "Moses, you are being released by way of a D.A. rejection. That means the district attorney did not buy into what they said they had on me. I knew I wasn't going home because when on parole even when the case is dropped you have to go in front of the board to have your case reviewed to see if you violated your conditions of parole. But on this day that didn't happen.

After I was taken to the property room and given my personal things, I was let out the front door of the police station. I didn't move for at least two minutes; I mean, I stood right there on the porch of the station because I knew this was a set-up to kill me. When nothing happened, I told myself that they made a mistake by letting me go while on parole. My criminal instincts kicked in, and I told myself that I damned sure wasn't going back in there and say, "Excuse me, you shouldn't have let me out because I'm on CYA parole."

They found out about the warrant out for me in Los Angeles from my fingerprints. I knew I was headed back to CYA or maybe even prison due to the fact I was now eighteen. I excepted a plea agreement for six months county time for the robbery. So, Los Angeles was going to have to wait until I finished serving my jail sentence. I went to San Diego and hooked up with a friend of mine from CYA, Rodney Randle. A few days later, we were arrested for robbery.

I was informed that I would not be going back to Los Angeles, but I was to be transferred to CYA for a parole hearing. I was happy about that, because this meant the assault charge on the housing authority police was not going to be refiled. Now, I was only looking at a one-year to eighteen-month violation of parole.

When I got back to the California Youth Authority, the year was 1975. It took thirty-two days for them to have my hearing. And just like I expected, I was given eighteen months. This time I was sent to YTS, which stands for Youth Training School. This place was known for housing all the hardcore, out-of-control teenagers.

The people I saw when I got there made me think that they had solved the gang problem in Los Angeles, because it seemed like we were all there. Just from my neighborhood alone there was Rickey Taylor a.k.a. Hardrock, Bingo, Mario Gray, Wendy Bruce, Neal Mattews, Micheal Ford, Junior Thomas, Tony Baker, and Larry Jackson. I had been stuck in the San Diego County Jail, and I didn't know that they had all got busted. We were all from the Nickerson Garden Bounty Hunter Blood Gang.

I also ran into some of our gang's closest allies, like Lorenzo Benton a.k.a. L.B., A.C. Moses a.k.a. King Bobalouie, Big Vincent, Big Savage, O.G. Bird, and a host of others that I met while serving my time. All these guys were there from Compton Piru Blood Gang: Cool Breeze, Cat Nip, and Pudding (who's resting in peace). The Crip gang outnumbered us on the streets, and it was no different in jail. Wanye Daye a.k.a. Baby honcho, Mack Thomas, J.J., U.T., Crazy Crip, Big Hercules, Micheal Gibson, Hoover Joe, Big Suger Bear, Cowboy, Jemmel, And Bull Dog. Damn, nearly every last one of the Crips mentioned represented a different Crip gang in Los Angeles.

The place was like a time bomb set to go off every time we saw each other. Most everyone that was mentioned were major factors in their gang. So, you would think with all of us off the streets at the same time the gang situation would be under control. But that was not the case because as fast as they locked up a gang member, new ones just kept emerging and new gangs continued to come out.

I was paroled in June of 1976, and when I returned to Los Angeles, I noticed that damn near every block in the inner city had a new gang in it.

My troubles continued with the police immediately upon my release. I started selling the drug heroin with some of my homeboys as soon as I got out.

One day. the police came into the parking lot and told me to get into the car just straight out of the blue. I looked at them like they were high on something and told them I wasn't getting in the car, because I hadn't done a damn thing. I was famous for breaking and running from the police, but this time I was clean so I stood my ground. They grabbed me and placed handcuffs on me. Once in the car, I said, "Man, I just got out. What is this all about?"

The police driving told me to just "shut the fuck up; you'll find out soon enough." That was true because all they did was drive me right across the street from the projects, and then park behind an unmarked cop car. Two plainclothes cops got out of the car and approached the car I was in. One of them opened the back door, and then looked me right in the face but said not a word. I didn't say anything either.

The cop that had put the cuffs on me said, "Hey, Moses, do you know who that guy is?"

I said, "No, why should I?"

He responded by saying "Because that's the guy you shot."

I was stunned and at a loss for words. When I finally replied, I looked the guy right in the face and said I was never convicted for that shooting. I also told him that it seems like every time somebody got shot I get blamed for it. Then surprisingly, one of the cops said, "You can go now."

They took the handcuffs off then said "We just wanted to let the guy you shot get a good look at you."

Before I walked away, I looked at the cop one more time and said, "Man, I didn't shoot you."

I was well known for carrying a gun on me, but during this period in my life I had stopped, because I was getting pulled over by the police every time they saw me. Also, I figured they were waiting for an opportunity like that to catch me with a gun so they would have an excuse to take me out. I was in one of those situations where you'd say "Well, you made the bed, now you have to lie in it." I say that because my reputation for carrying a gun and using it dates back to the late 1960s, so, when the Bloods and Crips gangs hit the streets, I was already known around the neighborhood for packing heat (gun).

Everything went smooth for me for about two months. Then one late night, I was sitting on my car talking to my girlfriend at the time, Monica Ford, when the entire parking lot filled up with police cars. I mean they came in there like they knew exactly who they were looking for. I just sat there because they were just sitting in their cars. Then two detectives came walking up from the back of all the cars; they walked right up to me. They never pulled out a gun.

One of them said, "Terry Moses, you are under arrest for murder." Then they led me away.

I asked them who was I supposed to have murdered this time. I didn't get a response. When we got to the station, I was booked for murder and then questioned about another murder. I had nothing to say about either one. All I wanted was a lawyer, because I was getting sick of this shit, and this madness was going to have to stop.

Again I was on parole and would have to answer to the board even if the charges is dismissed. Well, that's exactly what happened, charges dismissed. Now, I only had to deal with the parole violation.

In the year 1974, I did something that paid off for me in the long run. I had told my parole officer that I had been a target for any crime that took place because of my reputation. Well, he remembered that conversation. When it was time for my hearing, he informed the board that I had been arrested several times for murders that were dismissed. He went on to say that it seemed like I was being targeted by the police. He recommended that I be taken off parole, because he felt that I had been falsely accused each time. It felt good to have someone believe me for a change. I was released and discharged from parole thirty days later.

The year 1977 rolled in, and I was still on the streets. A new police station had been opened and the cops were all new. I felt relieved because every cop from the Seventy-Seventh Street Division knew who I was. I wasn't an active gang member anymore but that could have changed any second, because although you may not be active, your rivals still were and that meant your life was still in danger.

I was selling drugs on a rather large level in the beginning of 1978, when I got arrested for possession of cocaine and PCP. The new police station was now open so I wouldn't have to see all those cops that knew me. The new police station was called Southeast Division, and they were now in charge of patrolling the now gang-infested Watts area. Once I was booked in, I started making calls to get bailed out. That was another good thing about being off parole; you can bail out. I got in touch with Cassidy Bail Bonds and was waiting to be released.

I was feeling good about being able to bail out when the cell door opened up. It was two detectives that knew me from the early seventies. The first thing that was said was, "We heard you were still alive." They laughed a little, and then started asking me about the whereabouts of some of my homeboys, like Joe Barker, Gary Barker, and a few other well known Bounty Hunter gang members.

Then they called a few of the cops over to the cell. When they got there, one of the detectives said, "You guys take a good look at that face in there and remember it, because he is one of the Bounty Hunters that used to shoot at the LAPD."

I started to defend myself by telling these rookies I never was convicted of the crimes they are speaking about, but I thought better of it and just kicked back and hoped it doesn't get any worse.

They finally shut the door, leaving me alone. Ten minutes later, the door opened up again. This time it was the two young cops with one more behind them. Now, I knew they were up to no good because they had taken off their shirts with their badges on it.

The youngest of the three said to me, "Come on, Moses, we have to take your picture again."

I said, "No, thank you. I think you have enough pictures of me already." That made all three of them come in on me. They grabbed me and really took me to the photo room. Once they got me in the chair, one of the cops kicked me clear out of it. Now, I'm on the floor getting kicked everywhere except the face. They were talking to me while kicking the shit out of me, telling me what else was going to happen to me if I kept fucking with the LAPD.

When they were done, I was hauled back to the cell that they had taken me from. I was called for bail about an hour later. I left that police station feeling like a time bomb. I wanted to kill and if I said I felt any other way, I would be telling a fat ass lie. I was hurting all over.

When I did get home, I didn't come outside for over a week, and it wasn't because I was still hurt. It was so I would not lose control of myself and start fighting a battle that would have surely ended with me losing my life.

Thought of a Broken Man

Life starts off in a broken home,
know dreams just reality of everyday fatalities
and no one can feel your pain
because everybody in the ghetto is suffering the same.
You make a vow to yourself that when you get old
that shit was going to change,
but then your next endeavor turns out to be
the neighborhood street gang, now in your life
things are going backwards,
because the struggle you're in is
senseless and disastrous, so you curse
God feeling like a volcano ready to erupt
thinking could shit in life get much worse,
while the voices in your head
are saying maybe you are cursed,
you pick up your pistol and examine it
while it's in your hand,
then you look out the window and
see your thirteen-year-old sister
talking to a grown ass man.
Insanity or reality but the only thing
for certain is the next move
I make will result in a tragedy.

Chapter 12

A Day in Life

My introduction to the gang in my hood (neighborhood) was at the age of 15. At the time I was into graffiti heavily but I always kicked it with the homie Ty-budd from two P's (Pocoima Piru Gang). We mostly got drunk and talked to women. Then one day, the big homie Bubbles Blood took me to the hood. From there I started sagging my pants and claiming the Pocoima Piru Gang. It wasn't long before I caught a fool from the other side (rival gang). He was out of pocket (on rival turf) riding a beach cruiser. So, I asked one of the homies who was he, and he said that's the dude from up the hill (Crip hood) who was bragging about being a Crip.

So, I laid in wait behind some bushes until he came in range, and when he did, I caught him with a right hook. He flew off the bike and as soon as he got up, I said, "What's up, Blood?" He was scared to death, so, I took his bike and sold it for some bhronic (high quality weed). After that, you can say I was on hood patrol, hitting up (approaching) everybody who came down Pierce Street and Glenoaks.

I still remember the time I hit up this mark (perpetrator). The homies were selling drugs when we notice an intruder walking past the hood. I approached him and asked "Where are you from?" He tried to say he was from the hood but nobody knew him. So, we walked him back to the spot (hang-out place) and asked the big homie Arn Dog did he know him. As soon as he said no, I asked the mark for a fade (fight). Before he could get off a punch, I knocked him clear out of his shoes and ran him out of the hood. And from that day until now, I haven' t seen him since.

I slowly graduated to robbing houses, cars, and people, until one of the homies gave me a gun. Around that time, we were at war with the Mexicans. The reason why was because they had shot the homie Shack, plus they had shot and killed Garret, a non-affiliated, who was passing by on a scooter.

I wanted to test the strap (gun), so one night I got high and drove past the park where the Mexicans be. I got off a couple of rounds and sped off. No one was hit but it felt good to bust a heat (shoot a gun).

By the way, my name is Marlon but the Piru gang calls me Ak. The city is Pacomia, California, and it became infamous in the late 70s and early 80s with a spot called Sherm Alley. Throughout the city, the name rung synonymous with drugs and murder. Another popular spot was the Van Nuys Apartments also known as "Nam's," short for Vietnam, a place that got its name through violence and wild shootouts. It is connected to Pierce Park Apartments, which is known as Sherm Alley. Together they form the Van Nuys Apartments or (V.N.P.P.). This is my home. I grew up on empty shells and victims, where most die before the age of 25 due to gang warfare. The big homies would get locked up and when they got out they would lace (teach) the young homies and give them structure and in return, we would sell drugs and put in work for the hood.

Bloods and Crips The Genesis of a Genocide

It was a incident in particular when a young soldier from the hood took the bus to Poly High and killed a rival gang member. There also been other incidents where rivals were murdered inside of schools. Like in the mid-90s, a baby gangster by the name of Insane was convicted after being placed on America's Most Wanted for the shooting death of a young man inside of Maclay High.

There've been times when innocent people were caught in the crossfire. Like my sister, who was shot outside my apartment by two Crips who were trying to kill my homeboys Low Down and Kejuan. My sister was hit while she was throwing a young child out of harm's way. The two homies got away unharmed. To this day there are still bullet holes in my mother's stairs.

But the most memorable time in my history is when a young girl was killed at the Boys and Girls Club. Her name was Tiffany, and she was murdered when some Crips walked in the club and started shooting at some rival gang members. They missed them and hit Tiffany.

A lot of families were affected by this senseless killing. Parents stopped allowing their kids to go to the Boys and Girls Club. There was so much drama in the city, the war between the Crips and Bloods was at a all time high. Brothers were getting murdered for little or nothing; having the wrong color on was a reason to get shot.

Some were murdered while trying to attack their rivals, like the time a Crip was murdered in our building after running into the building to shoot at some rival gang members, and then getting lost in the endless maze that makes up our apartment building.

That reminds me; the same day my sister was shot, later that night one of the O.G.s (original gangster) from my hood was shot while crossing the street of the park in Lakeview Terrace (Lakeview Terrace is also the place of the Rodney King beating). His name was Perm Dogg. After the death of Perm Dogg, the whole neighborhood went into mourning with R.I.P. (rest in peace) shirts, revenge, and the traditional pouring out liquor to honor the dead homie. We later renamed the park Perm Park in memory of his death.

Still little changed. The homie Bubbles Blood left shortly after bringing me to the hood. He ended up getting locked up in Las Vegas for robbery. So, it was just me and Little Ty Budd until we got arrested for assault and battery at a local grocery store. Little Ty Budd beat his case, but mine was more serious because I was caught stomping the head of one the men when the police arrived. I pleaded no contest to an assault and battery and was given three years' probation.

Not long after that, Little Ty Budd moved out of the apartments. I was left to run wild until the big homie El Dogg was released from prison. After he was paroled, we became inseparable. We would ride around all day high on PCP while we gambled and tried to have sex with the ladies. It didn't take long for El Dogg to resume his roll as a ridah (one who puts in work) in the hood. Whether it was at the club fighting, bouncing out of vehicles, or busting (shooting) at muthafuckas. He pushed the Pacomia Piru line to the fullest. He inspired me to become more active.

Like the time we saw a rival wearing all blue coming out of a liquor store. Just so happens he was closer to the driver side so I gave the wheel to El Dogg and jumped out and said "What that Piru like?" He ran into a church, so I gave up pursuit and ran back to the car. That's just a example of how my mentality had changed. It could be on sight; it didn't matter where.

Soon after El Dogg was released, we started hooking up with some more of our homies that were fresh out of the penitentary, like Wimpru, Little Dx Krazy, and Big Pooh Ridah. We formed a B.G. (Baby gangster) headquarters in

Bloods and Crips The Genesis of a Genocide

enemy territory. It was nothing to us to walk hard down the street flamed up (wearing all red), daring anybody to step up to us. We caught a few rivals slipping on their own turf, like the day me and the homies caught a rival gang member at the bus stop. We made a u-turn and ran up on him while he was boarding the bus. We stomped him out in broad daylight and jetted (ran) back to the hood.

There've been many occasions when we have been caught off-guard that ended fatally, like in the case of Little Bebo who was shot in the head and killed in a hallway of a apartment building.

But the streets isn't the only place you can get caught up, the little homie Lobo was beaten into a coma during a riot at Wayside County Jail in Los Angeles. He later died from the injuries. El Dogg and I was nearly killed at a fast food restaurant called Keyes by some Crips passing in the opposite lane.

But one of the things that stands out in my mind is the shooting at the crack house (cocaine house). That day all was well; the homies were making money when one of the smokers (cocaine user) had come to buy some dope to get high. Little did we know that he had just stolen a TV from his own sister. So, she knocked on the door and when he answered, she shot him in the face, This is sad, but this is a rough example of how drugs have impacted our community. Po, El Dogg and I began smoking a lot of sherm (PCP) that eventually led to him getting violated.

While he was gone, I continued to get into trouble. In the same lot I was arrested in, me and a couple of homies found ourselves in an altercation with some guards. A Pisa (border brother) accused us of trying to rob him. So, the guards tried to apprehend us. One of the guards was a rival gang member. So, when he tried to question us I spit in his face. That ignited an all-out fight between us. I was struck by a Mexican in the crowd when we started getting the best of the guards. It ended with us getting pepper sprayed and running from the scene before the cops came.

It wasn't long before the Big homie El Dogg was free. He made a little homie (portage) while he was in jail, a young soldier that he named Little El Dogg. So, once again we became inseparable, eating spreads (jailhouse-style meals) and smoking water (PCP). As you can see, he hadn't changed or learned a thing. His time behind the wall (incarcerated) just made him more hardened.

It's a trip how this gang thang revolved. In the beginning we were a union. We're all branches off the original Piru gang in West Side Compton, California, on Piru Street. Before all of the genocide, we were known by a Powerful Invincible Righteous Union acronym, which was P.I.R.U. So, as time went on we kept losing our homeboys to the system. A lot of us were getting struck out (three strikes) when others were getting life for murder.

Then the day came when me and the homie El Dogg were getting faded (drunk) off eight ball (old English) and lovely (weed mixed with PCP). As he continued to smoke and down the eight ball, he began to act strange. What I mean is, he started flashing gang signs at every car that passed by, saying that they were either mad dogging (staring down at him) or were enemies.

I tried to calm him down but he wasn't having it. He started calling me a crab (derogatory word for Crip), telling me I couldn't be in the hood and he was going to kill me. He tried to smash a bottle over my head. I removed my blunt cutter (cigar cutter) from my pocket and stabbed him in the shoulder as he swung the bottle at my head. I was then caught with a right cross and knocked over the fence. As I got up, a small scuffle ensued. My shirt was torn off in the struggle as I found myself in a chokehold with the big homie trying to choke the life out of me. I stabbed him several times before he collapsed.

My mother immediately began performing CPR, as I kept talking to him in desperate hopes of keeping him awake to prevent him from going into shock. I waited with him until the cops arrived. I kissed him on the head and told him that I loved him but I got to go to jail.

Later that night I got the news from the officer that El Dogg died in the hospital. I was heartbroken, but during the trial I found out that he had consumed so much PCP that it had became toxic.

I was sentenced to prison for manslaughter, which I'm still serving time on.

Dear reader, it was very important for me to express my former lifestyle exactly the way it was, uncut raw and self destructive. The conclusion of me taking my friend's life shows that anything can and will happen if you choose to trap yourself in an uncontrollable lifestyle. I feel the pain every single day and will have to live with that regret for the rest of my life.

So, I truly hope and pray that whichever youngsters get the opportunity to read my story understand that the outcome of this type of life is always fatal. Thank you for reading a day in my life.

Hallucinating

For just a few minutes I believed I could fly,
until the wind blew and slapped reality
back into my face, then I was scared shitless
with nothing to say
wondering how in the hell did I get up
on this building any goddamn way,
but maybe it was the PCP
I smoked earlier that day,
but I really couldn't say,
when I finally did make it down there
was people standing all around,
and for some strange reason
I was flat on the ground
and my body wouldn't move and
my arms or legs I was unable to use,
something wasn't right because
just a minute ago or two,
when the wind blew
I was sure I knew exactly what to do,
or did I just imagine that I was okay
then jumped any goddamn way.

Chapter 13

Crack Cocaine, PCP, and Gangs

It has been said throughout history that money is the root of all evil. I personally agree, and you probably will after you have witnessed what money and power did to some of the most notorious gangs and their members in the city of Los Angeles and beyond. First, I need you to understand that when the Blood and Crip gangs took to the streets in the early 1970s, there was complete dedication to the gang. As mentioned, the gang's reputation meant more to us than getting an education.

But in the mid-1970s, something happened that changed all that, and plain and simply said it was dope and money. I mean crack cocaine and PCP, also known in legal terms as phencyclidine. Those two drugs dominated the streets and the minds of everybody that came in contact with them. Money, power, addiction, and greed turned the gang's loyalty into envy and hate for their own fellow gang members.

Some of the things that happened to people that I personally knew you would see only in a horror movie. When I started manufacturing PCP in the mid-1970s, I saw the power that money brought. People would do anything for you from store earns to murder. I use to give some of my friends PCP to sell for me so they could make some money for themselves as well.

In 1980, when I was still recovering from a PCP lab explosion in which one of my best friends died, I started giving Leonard Thompson, who is a childhood friend, some PCP to sell to get back on his feet. He had just gotten out of the Los Angeles County Jail where he had been acquitted for a murder charge. He had gone to Texas to stand trial. When the case was won, he decided to stay in California.

He had gotten married while in Texas and had two kids by a Alabama girl name Mattie. So, with his family, I was reluctant at first to give him the drug, because I remembered that he used to smoke the stuff and go on some way-out trips, but he assured me that he was not going to indulge anymore. So, I gave him a jug of the very powerful and hallucinating shit. I told him I would come by in a few days to see if he needed some more.

Three days passed before I went back to the projects and when I finally did, the news wasn't good at all. I knocked on the door and when Mattie answered, she had a real strange look on her face, a look of hurt and fear. I said, "Mattie, what's wrong?"

She told me to come in. She said, "Last night Stan shot Leonard then killed his self." I said "Damn" out loud. She then said Leonard had been shot five times and was still hanging onto life.

She started telling me what happened from the beginning. She said Stan and Leonard were out in the parking lot selling PCP when they decided to call it a night. Now, Stan was staying with Leonard at the time because he had no place to stay. So, Leonard was nice enough to let him sleep on the couch until he was able to do better for his-self.

Bloods and Crips The Genesis of a Genocide

Once in the apartment, Leonard made a pitcher of Kool-Aid and went upstairs with Mattie and the kids.

After Leonard was up stairs for a few minutes, Stan started to call to him. Leonard told Stan that he would be down later because he was watching TV. Stan insisted, saying "Man, it's important." So, Leonard went to the stairs to make his way down to see what Stan wanted. When he took one step down, he looked and saw Stan pointing a pistol up at him. Before he could retreat to safety, Stan started shooting. Stan shot him five times missing him only once at close range.

Mattie said she ran to the top of the stairs and saw that Leonard had fallen all the way down and Stan was standing over him clicking the empty pistol, as if to keep shooting Leonard.

When Stan realized that the gun was empty he ran into the kitchen and grabbed Leonard's double-barreled shotgun that Mattie had brought from Texas when they came out here to California.

When Mattie saw Stan getting ready to finish Leonard off with the shotgun, she started screaming at him, "Stan, no, don't do it! Please, Stan, don't do it!"

Mattie said when Stan looked at her it was like he was looking at her for the first time. Then he looked at the shotgun in his hand, and then down at Leonard. She said when she saw that he was confused, she made her way down to him and started pushing him towards the door. This took a lot of heart seeing that he had just shot her husband and was still holding a double-barreled shotgun.

She said he responded by backing up each time she would push him. When she got him to the back door of the apartment she pushed him out and closed the door. She then ran back to where Leonard was. He was still alive laying on his back looking up into her eyes. All of a sudden, she heard a very loud blast from outside the apartment, so after she called 911 for Leonard, she looked out the back door to see Stan laying dead with most of his head shot off.

Now, sitting there in complete shock, I started to feel somewhat responsible because it was me who had given Leonard the PCP, and Mattie had told me during our conversation that they, in fact, had been smoking some. I asked Mattie did she want me to take her to the hospital to see him. I wanted to see him as well.

When we got to the hospital, Leonard was awake and fusing with one of the nurses. We knew then that he was going to survive being shot five times. When we started to talk, he told me the he wished Stan would have at least stayed alive long enough to tell him why the fuck he had shot him. I told him that "we would never know the answer to that, but just be thankful that you pulled through."

The PCP had taken control of the situation, making Leonard a enemy in Stan's mind. Whatever it was that he was thinking made him want to kill, and once he came somewhat to his senses and realized what he had done, he took his own life.

This is the deadly combination that the gangs collaborated with. Some smoked it to become the greatest gangbanging killers of all time. While others like myself wanted to get rich from the deadly poison. This manmade drug brought power, money, and madness to the Crips and Blood gangs.

It only got worst when the crack epidemic came into the picture in the early 1980s. This is when the gang's dedication deteriorated. Same gang killings started to happen because of the money mixed with the madness. Gangs started forming small crews within the gangs to sell drugs which caused chaos amongst the gangbangers from that same gang that stayed true to just gangbanging.

Bloods and Crips The Genesis of a Genocide

What we all found out was that there was no loyalty when it came to money amongst the gangs. Guys with the money started to feel threatened by their own. So guys would be found dead, and the blame would go to the rival enemy, causing that gang to be retaliated against for something they didn't even do. You had gang members starting small empires from drug money and were being protected by the gangs.

Third World was a crew made up of gang members that were very ruthless about getting paid and protecting their interest. Whitey Enterprises was another gang that went to war with Third World, and the killings were listed as gang killings but over drug money and territory. Freeway Rick: it was once said that he bailed out of a Hollywood police station with a million dollars in cash. He stayed in the news because he had become a giant in the drug world, but was still considered a Crip gang member. This type of fame for gang members caused them to become the biggest targets in the city. I mean that literally, because now the police knew who you are. The rival gangs still wanted to kill you, and now your own gang was plotting on you because they wanted what you had. It was a losing situation, and the results are the evidence of this truth.

By the year 1981, things really started to get low down and dirtier than it already was. This guy I went to school with name Neal Clark was the first one that I knew personally that fell victim to the new way of things that were being done. The story is short with this brother because his body has never been found to this very day. Vanished, without a trace. In 1983, a young guy name Ronald, a.k.a. Wizard, also came up missing, and his body, like Neal's, has never been found.

Things had changed in the gang/drug life, because there was now so much money involved that the people closest to you were the ones you had to watch. Neal Clark was from the Imperial Courts Projects in Watts, while Wizard was from the Nickerson Garden Projects also in Watts. They both are still considered missing because their bodies have never been found but nobody believed that they were still missing. Shit, everybody in the streets knew how dead serious, lowdown, and dirty the game, so to speak, was being played.

The beginning of the 1990s was even more tragic for gang members turning into drug dealers. In Watts, because the hate and envy was running dangerously deep, a new way of killing was coming about. Rene McCowan had made a few million dollars and was well known all over the City of Los Angeles as one of the major players in the drug game. Well, he was up-ducted in early 1991 and when his body was found, it wasn't nice. He had been decapitated and brutalized for all to see.

Micheal Bell, another well known gang member who turned dope dealer, was snatched off the streets by whoever wanted him dead and was also said to have been decapitated. Micheal Bell, a.k.a. Cyclone was from the Miller Gangster Blood Gang, not yet thirty years old when he died. Billy Ray from the Jordan Down Projects Grape Street Crip Gang, met the same kind of ending as Rene and Cyclone. It was like whoever did these vicious killings was leaving a message of some kind of how you would now die if you crossed whoever they were.

These incidents spoken about are only a small portion of what was going on all over the State of California behind drugs affiliated with gangs, particularly with the Bloods and Crips. Life goes on for us who have lived through this type of lifestyle but the memories of what happened to these guys will forever be with us because it could have happened to any one of us the same exact way.

Chapter 14

Haze

"What's up, Cuzz?"

For the last sixteen of my thirty years living, that has been my greeting. My name is Shannon Johnson, a.k.a. (also know as) Badnews. And for me, it all began on the west side of Pomona, California in the Crip neighborhood they call Tray Five Seven. I remember when I was first introduced to the word "Cuzz." I was fourteen years old. Me and my homeboys Tiny Moe and Cartoon were smoking PCP in an abandoned house in the neighborhood when Cartoon said, "Pass me the stick, Cuzz." (PCP stick)

I freaked, because I knew that the word "Cuzz" was associated with the Crip gang. I asked Cartoon was he a Crip.

He replied, "Hell, yeah, Cuzz, I'm a Crip. You need to be one, too. You grew up in the hood (neighborhood) all your life; to me you are a Crip." He then went on to say "As a matter of fact, we're going to make it official." He called in some more homeboys who surrounded me and began to hit me. This was my initiation into the West Side Tray Five Seven Crip Gang.

Reflecting back, I realize I was under the influence of PCP practically all of my life. I was walking in an intoxicated haze and believe me when I say at times it feel like I still am.

There was this one time when I was looped up (intoxicated). One of my homeboys had dared me to jump in a car that was at a gas station. The owner of the car was pumping the gas, so, being me, I jumped in the car and sped away while the owner was holding the gas hose.

I used to do stupid shit like that all the time. I can't blame it all on the drugs, because a lot of it had to do with the type of life I was living.

The crazy thing about it, I thought I was having fun. My perception of life was twisted. I even thought getting jumped was fun. It proved how down I was. For instance, I was enrolled in Pomona High School, Now, this is an all-Blood school, so me being a Crip was all bad. I told my grandmother I couldn't go to that school. Since I'd been kicked out of three previous schools, she wasn't hearing it. But she soon found out I was telling the truth because I didn't make it to class. Four Bloods jumped me, and I didn't have a chance. All I thought about was revenge. So I went to my homeboy's house, got a gun, and shot up the school. I was lucky no one was hit.

After that, I was kicked out of the Pomona School District. I had to go to school in San Bernadino, and I brought the drama with me. By this time I was Crip-crazy; you couldn't tell me shit. It was Crip or nothing. In reality, I was losing my mind. PCP and this gang life had me. My grandmother would look at me and shake her head. I didn't care though. All I wanted to do was smoke sherm (PCP) and gangbang. And, after that, they found my uncle's body lying in an alley, all I wanted to do was kill, especially when

Bloods and Crips The Genesis of a Genocide

it came out that the Bloods were responsible. This just fueled my decision that the red rags (Bloods) were my true and only enemy.

I couldn't grasp the concept that the people responsible for killing my uncle was me. Let me explain. If I grab a gun and shoot someone just because he's wearing the color red, then I am the same as the one who shot my uncle, because they killed him because he was a Crip. There's no difference but at the time, my mind was so polluted and I was so trapped in that life, I was blind. I wanted an eye for an eye, and sometimes just an eye.

I remember when I saw my first dead body. I was at a party in my neighborhood when my homeboy Greg started arguing with a female from another Crip neighborhood. One of her homeboys produced a gun and started shooting. A body dropped, but it wasn't Greg. Chaos broke out. Everybody started screaming and running, and I remember looking at the body lying on the floor. I didn't know the person, nor did I care. All I cared about was revenge. These fools had the nerve to shoot up our neighborhood party. I was going to make sure there would be a payback.

But before a payback could be had, I was arrested for a burglary. The purpose of the burglary was to acquire guns. The Lord works in mysterious ways, because prior to the burglary we had found out where the dude who fired the shots stayed, so we knew where to find him. Instead of a burglary, it could have been a murder.

Now, I'm locked up with no way out. I was placed in the Crip module. For those of you who are not familiar with the Los Angeles County Jail system, the Crip module is where they put all the active Crips. The gang violence between the Crips and Bloods is so volatile, they have to separate the two.

Now, the Crip module is a world of its own. You would think, since everyone is a Crip, it would be peace and harmony. It's just the opposite. You see, most Crip gangs' worst enemies are other Crips. This produces a lot of Crip-on-Crip violence, especially in the modules. So they have to separate the Crips by their neighborhoods.

I know first hand about the violence, because I was jumped by some East Coast and Hoover Crips the very first night. It all started over words, and next thing you know I'm on the ground getting kicked. The fight was broken up by the sheriffs, and we were separated. I was placed on a row (tier) with other Crips from my neighborhood. I let everyone know what had happened, and let them know what I wanted done. I wanted revenge.

This is the life of a Crip in the module. Enemies are created over colors and words. I have seen people robbed, stabbed, and raped in this place.

I remember one night when we were going back and forth busting on each other (talking trash). This one dude got mad because the homie from the hood was getting the best of him. So he decided to get bold and diss the hood (a derogatory remark against the neighborhood). Everyone got quiet. The fun was over. Before another word was spoken, we heard the dude hollering. The homie that was in the cell with him was putting hands on him (beating him). The homie made him get naked. To make a long story short, let's just say the dude's name was Sam, but by the morning his name was Samantha.

I can tell you all types of stories about the module. As a matter of fact, I can fill up a whole book. I'm glad each time I was there my stay was short. Like, this time I was only there for three days. When I got out, all I thought about was getting wet (high on PCP), as usual. But was I broke. I didn't have a dime to my name. So I had to figure out a way to get some fast cash. I couldn't sell drugs, because I didn't have the patience for it. So, I resorted back to my preferred trade, robbery.

Like I said, I was broke, so I couldn't afford a gun. I had to be resourceful. I grabbed a two-by-four with a nail in it and went to a 7-11 convenience store. I walked in, approached the cashier, and demanded the money. I guess he wasn't scared of the two-by-four, because his response was "Get the hell out of here."

When I saw he wasn't going to bulge, I did just that and got the hell out of there. Now I was really desperate.

I hooked up with one of my homeboys and Lord behold, he had a gun. Now I'm in business. We went to a restaurant, and as soon as I stepped in, I shot in the air. This got everyone's attention. I demanded the money from the cashier who had no problem complying. As soon as I got the money, me and the homie ran out of there. We thought we had gotten away, but a police car was pulling into the parking lot with their sirens on. The police told us to freeze and get on the ground. Once again, I'm on my way back to County. Now, as I sit in this cell reflecting on all that has happened in my life, I can clearly see the pain I have caused.

When I look at my grandmother and think about all she has been through dealing with me and my brothers and sisters, I ask myself, have I ever given her a reason to smile? I may have, but I had to be awfully young, because I sure can't remember. And it hurts.

So those of you who still have a chance to live, live. Don't go down this road. Because all this road leads to is the land of regrets. For me, it's time for a dramatic change. It's time to put that smile back on my grandmother's face and clear my conscience of the unjustified hate I've carried around for too many years.

Ghetto Love

I was born and raised in the ghetto
but still remained a child of God.
My grandmother taught me this
even though times were tough and mighty hard, she provided the best she could
and constantly said that God was good.
She cried a lot which is something I'll never forget, but when she smiled it made me
awfully proud to be her grandchild.
So, dear Lord, please hear my prayer
for a grandmother who has always been there,
she doesn't ask for much
just enough to see us through,
and even then her praise and glory is
still all for you.
So, my prayer to you is to help
Grandmother to see us through,
because through all the trials and tribulations
of life in the ghetto, through the tears and
all the hard years, she stood tall
and refused to let us fall.
She is a grandmother like no other
that I place no one above her and there's
not enough words
to express the love that is truly felt for her.

Chapter 15

Operation Safe Streets

By the year 1982, it was obvious that the Crips and Bloods had grown so large that not only did law enforcement have a major problem with them on the streets, but now the Los Angeles County Jail had become a battleground for these gangs. So the L.A. County sheriffs decided to separate the gangs completely once they were arrested and identified as gang members. They were placed in what they called the gang module. The Blood gangs started calling the one they were in the Blood Module and the Crips called theirs the Crip Module. With that said, a brand new era of hatred, self destruction, and corruption was born. This new way of battling gang violence was titled O.S.S., which stands for "OPERATION SAFE STREET."

Once you are placed in one of the gang modules, you are then shackled up every time you have to be moved, just like a person on death row. Some of the things that went on in these gang modules back then are the very reason a lot of the Blood gangs don't get along as allies as they once did. The same thing applies to Crip gangs. Once they started locking the gangs up together they started turning on each other. What has to be remembered is these gangs just carried the same name, but they had come from all over Los Angeles into this gang module, and most of them were seeing each other for the very first time in life.

In the early 1970s, there was the Eastside Crips and the Westside Crips, but they then branched off and started forming gangs like the Kitchen Crips and the Qute 102 Crips, both from the east side of Los Angeles; and on the west side of Los Angeles the same thing was happening. Gangs on the west side branched off like the Hoover Crips, Underground Crips, or the Harlem Godfather Crips. That's just to name a few, but by the time the eighties arrived there were at least twenty-five or thirty different Crip gangs in Los Angeles.

The Blood gangs, who fought against the Crips, had the same exact thing happening to them. Bloods from Pomona, Compton, Watts, and the west side of Los Angeles came in contact with each other because of the gang module. Most of these gangs used to hear about what the other gangs had done, but never really socialized with one another on a get-to-know each other basis.

The L.A. County sheriffs, who were in charge of these modules, committed just as many felonies as the gang members. And if you got on the bad side of the sheriffs, no matter if you were a Crip or Blood, the results were always fatal. There were times when we would be in the gang module dayroom for two hours of television and phone calls. Some times, the dayroom door would come open and a Crip gang member would be pushed into the dayroom, and the door would then be locked. The Crip would be immediately rushed and beat down until the sheriffs were satisfied. Then they would drag him out.

But believe me they did not discriminate because Blood gang members used to get the very same treatment when they pissed off the sheriffs. They did these kinds of things to guys for information or just because they could. As one of the originals, I confess that by the 1980s it was evident that this was something that had gotten much bigger than me. "Tookie" Williams, Raymond Washington, Jemel, James Miller, L.B. a.k.a. Lorenzo Benton, Puddin, China Dog, Barefoot Puggie, Monkieman, Junior Thomas, Wanye Daye, Author Daye a.k.a. Big Huncho and Baby Huncho, Mack Thomas, Crazy Crip, Ray Williams a.k.a. Frog, Hot Rod, Hoover Joe, Sugar Bear (the original one from Qute 102), Joe, Tony and Gary Barker, Santa Claus, The Originals from the San Diego Bloods and Crip gangs, Wackie He He, Wackie Kackie, Peanut, Schoolyard, Mad Blood, Finnie Boy, Top Cat, and all the other originals that were there in the beginning.

The Crip and Blood gangs got larger than any of us could have imagined they would, and I personally was unfortunate to be able to witness the change these gang modules had on the gangs. Don't get me wrong, because I will be the first one to say that the Crip and Blood self-destructive genocide was the stupidest thing I ever involved myself with.

But there is another side of the story that the general public knows nothing about. Like how a blood gang member used to be put in the wrong holding tank while at court, placed in a cell full of Crip gang members on purpose just to keep the flame of this hatred burning. Of course, that Blood gang member would be beaten to an inch of his life, while the county sheriffs would only report it as a mistake.

Now the first thing that's on the gang member's mind when he gets out is revenge. Mission accomplished by Operation Safe Street. Nobody cared what was going on in these gang modules, because it was supposed to be such a great idea to identify gang members and keep them off the streets. While the gangs that were suppose to be allies with each other were becoming enemies in these gang modules, the sheriffs in charge of Operation Safe Streets were busy finding other ways to divide and conquer. Sometimes I think they set people up just for recreation to see what would happen to the guy.

One time back in 1985, when the blood gangs were being housed in the 3600 gang module, they had like five telephones located in the hallway of the unit. Me and some other gang members were using the phones when the door to the unit opened up. They told this guy to set down while they did the paper work. All of a sudden one of the Bloods on the phone looked up at the guy and said "Blood, that's Cadillac Bob, that fool is a Crip."

Everybody on the telephones stopped talking and turned their attention to Cadillac Bob. He started to speak up for his self, saying that he never gangbanged, but lived in a Crip neighborhood. Then Frog from Neighborhood Twenties Blood gang came to his defense by saying "Man, he's right. Everybody knows this guy is a player. That's why they call him Cadillac Bob."

The sheriffs were nowhere in sight when this conversation took place. They would only come back after the person has been beaten down. But this time it didn't work. He refused to come in the module, and the Bloods refused to attack him. Now that was one of the few times that one of these set-ups didn't result in a guy getting his ass beat.

These tactics that the sheriff used worked because of the hatred that had already been embedded in the minds of the rival gangs, so it was always a violent reaction to these situations. There was so much drama created through these gang modules that you can ask some of the hardcore Crip gang members that went through the Forty-Eight Hundred Crip Module, who are their worst enemies? And some of the responses would be "Another Crip gang."

The fighting and stabbings in the Crip modules led to the streets, and after so many years of it, some of their worst enemies became Crip gangs not Blood gangs. While the Crips were busy turning on each other in Forty-Eight Hundred, the Bloods were doing the same thing in Forty-Three Hundred. Set tripping was the term everybody used back then. It meant that when one Blood gang out numbered another gang they would look for reasons to start a fight which would more than likely turn into a gang fight. And as mentioned, it escalated from the gang modules to the streets.

When I think about it now, I can vividly see the trap. But twenty-five years ago, I was just as blind as everyone else. It got so bad at one time in the Crip module that they had to be separated from each other by being placed in one-man cells. The incident that brought this about was when a guy in the Crip module was tied up, then put in a bed cover and set on fire. Assaults and even rapes started to occur in the Crip and Blood modules. This place became so brutal that when a person gets jumped on in one of the cells they just holler "Man down," and the cops would open the cell gate and a bloody person would come staggering or sometimes even crawling down the tier. Now you need to remember that this was happening to guys who represented that same gang, Crips attacking Crips and Bloods attacking Bloods.

A question to be asked is who would be the beneficiary from this type of self destructive behavior? In my opinion, we became job security for the sheriffs and the LAPD. There is nothing that I can say good about these gang modules, because I saw and took part in so much bullshit that if I considered any of it good then I would be a insane fool.

Chapter 16

War Stories

"It never rains in Southern California." This was a hit song recorded in the early 1990s by the Oakland-based group Tony, Toni, Tone. I don't know the true meaning behind the words of this song, because, for one, it rains in Southern California and as far as the blacks dealing with the gang situation, it hails.

Speaking of hail, I hail from the southernmost tip or bottom of California in the City of San Diego. I would like to begin at the age of twelve, because prior to that age my life was pretty much uneventful. It all started for me in junior high. I was enrolled in Samuel Gompers High School on 47th and Hilltop. This school sits right dab in the middle of the gang-infested 47 Neighborhood Crip Gang territory. Even though this school was in a Crip neighborhood, there were a lot of Bloods going to this school. You had the L.P.B. (Lincoln Park Blood Gang), the E.H.B. (Emerald Hills Blood Gang), the L.A.P. (Little Afrika Piru Blood Gang), the 59 Brims Blood Gang, and the Skyline Eastside Piru Blood Gang. So gang violence was a normal occurrence.

I remember all the Damu's (Swahili word for Blood) would meet up at the west campus bathroom where we would beat box (make music with your mouth) rap, and talk shit. Well, I remember this one time when we were all ditching third period when the homie from L.P.B. ran in the bathroom and told us the homie 2bs was getting jumped by some rips (Crips) outside of Ms. Reynolds class.

Now, at this time I wasn't from a gang, even though I was hanging around with the Bloods. That mostly was due to my closest friends Karl Moore, Butter, Smiley Bo, and Wicked Weeze being Bloods. So, I chose to follow suit.

When we got to Ms. Reynold's class, we saw that the security guards had run everybody off and had taken 2bs to the nurse's office. This broke up our ditching because the security guards made us all go back to our classes. Not fifteen minutes later, we heard screaming coming from the walkway. When me and the homie Smiley Bo reached the walkway, we saw security guards rushing into one of the classrooms. We went to see what was going on. By the time we reached the class, the security guards were escorting Tutor from E.H.B. and the homie from L.A.P. (I can't remember his name) from the classroom.

After they brought them out, they brought out Junior from N.H.C. (Neighborhood Crip). I asked the homegirl Missy what happened. (She was in Tutor's class.) She said when the dude from L.A.P. walked in the class he approached Junior and punched him in the face. The next thing you know, Tutor joined in and they jumped Junior.

Once again, we were told to go back to our class. Nothing happened between then and lunch time. At lunch period, we all met up in front of the west campus cafeteria. Everybody was brought up to speed on what had happened. The school had called the police and they had taken Tutor and the homie from L.A.P. to Juvenile Hall. Everybody wanted to get off on the rips. We all decided to wait until after school.

Now, they had a lot of Crips going here, like the ones from N.H.C. Dant'e, Fatboy, Dicy, Cuzzy, Dukie Dave, Bayloc, Bullet Loco, Black Cuzz, Weasal, Bugz, Smokey, Red, Butner, Mickey, John, Junior, J.S, E-Dog, Greg, and Crip stick. They also had some of their homegirls going there as well, like Monique, Lady, Nykia, Toshee, Dalacia, and Kimmy. (There were a few more that I don't remember.) The Dumas were T bone, Mauzy a.k.a. M Hound, Wicked Weeze, Karl Moore a.k.a. Ck Bo, and Bontell. They were all from Lincoln Park Bloods. From E.H.B., you had Tutor, Fat Rabbit, and little L.O. From Skyline, it was Sergio Bailey, Butter, 2bs, John John, D Bo, Lamont, and L.B. (I can't remember the names of all the rest).

When school let out, there were around fifteen police cars in front of the school. So, nothing jumped off. As a matter of fact, everything was quiet until that Friday. During the lunch hour, a bunch of Crips bum-rushed the school. These weren't the Crips we were used to. They were huge. And they were knocking out everybody wearing red, green, or gray. We completely got caught off-guard. And I must say we got fucked up.

When the smoke cleared, you had people with broken jaws, noses, black eyes, and someone even got their arm broken. Even though we weren't responsible for the incident, a lot of us were kicked out.

I got enrolled into Keeler Middle school. This school was a Damu school, particularly the Skyline Eastside Piru Gang. You had Ronald Rush, Ty, John John, Nut, J Bick, Frank Nitti, Bill, Bugs, Barlos, Baby Ant, Joe Bowdie, Ty Bud, Heman, Daymond, Boo, Mike B, Baby E, Bo Bo, T Ru, Baby Holiday, Little Cowboy, and Tone.

We didn't have to worry about the Crips, because not only were there a lot of Bloods, but also the school was in

Blood territory. A lot of Damus didn't get that fortunate, because some were left at Gompers, like the homie Bontell, who got shot by a rival gang and was paralyzed from the waist down. The homie Wicked Weeze got jumped and beat severely by a rival gang on his way home from school. A lot of drama occurred at Gompers that year.

There were a lot going on in the southeast as well. The L.P.B. (Lincoln Park Bloods) were at war with some Los Angeles Crips who came to San Diego to set up shop, so to speak, with the drug trade. The L.P.B. gang had a click called S.Y.P. (Syndo Mobb), and they weren't having it. The drug epidemic hit the Southeast hard, and a lot of people got what we call "Hood Rich," which means they had the pretty cars, jewels, and a couple of thousand dollars in their pockets, but couldn't afford to leave the hood.

With this new found wealth came the guns. Everybody had a pistol, and everybody went gun crazy. This is when the drivebys got popular. A driveby is when you roll up on your enemy in a car and start shooting and drive off. I remember when I was first introduced to the driveby. It occurred at the mall called College Grove. A bunch of us were kicking it in front of the Gold Rush Arcade. It was me, Buster James, Smiley Bo, Mike Mike, Steve Nutty, Sick Ant, and a couple of females.

We were talking to the females when a car pulled up and said "What's up, Cuzz?" and immediately started busting (shooting). Everybody ran but a lot of people still got shot. Lucky I wasn't one of them. Me and Mike Mike met up by Chollas Lake. I asked him if he got a chance to get a shot off. He said no, he wasn't able to get to his gun in time.

We walked all the way to the homie Ron's house in North Park. It's like a 10-mile hike, so it was a journey. When we got to Ron's, we got in touch with Smiley Bo, who informed us that two of the females that we were talking to had gotten shot, but it wasn't life-threatening.

Bloods and Crips The Genesis of a Genocide

My crew immediately kicked off a war with the E.D.M. (East Diego Mob) and the West Coast Crips. It got so heated that a rival gang member came through Skyline and shot three of the homies with a semi-automatic gun in broad daylight. Later on that night, we went over to their hood and tore some shit up.

We were doing stupid shit like that which kept me in and out of Juvenile Hall. I was finally sent to CYA (California Youth Authority) for a ninety-day observation for assault with a deadly weapon. After my ninety days were up, the judge showed me mercy by allowing me to go to a program called Time Out instead of going back to CYA. It was more like a group home. It was located in the West Coast 30s Crip Gang territory. They had a few Crips in the group home. There was this one named Dawun a.k.a. D Loc, we use to get into it everyday, and not to be bragging, I use to get the best of him.

I had two more homies there with me named Mike Edmondson from Skyline and Larry Gist from Opharrol Park Bankster Blood Gang. The three of us used to terrorize the group home. I don't know how I successfully made it through the program, but I did.

When I was released, I was enrolled in a continuation school called Garfield. It was drama the first day. The movie "Colors" had just came out, and all the gang members were fired up. I remember we were all at the liquor store across the street from the school, when some neighborhood Crips came in. It was Dicey, Black Mike, Skipper, and Bay Loc. The homie Amid from Skyline and Black Mike started talking shit to one another. The next thing you know a fight broke out. We all ended up outside of the store where the vice principal tried to stop the fighting.

In the mist of the fighting, the vice principal got stabbed. We all looked up and saw the police who were getting out of their cars with their guns drawn. They told everybody to freeze. To make a long story short, a bunch of us got carried off to Juvenile Hall.

This was a drama week for me because I almost lost my life that following Saturday. I had just brought a Datsun 510 wagon from a Mexican, and I had to put it in the shop because it needed an alternator. When it was time for me to pick the car up from the shop, I was late due to Vershawn, my girl at the time. The shop was located on Fairmont street in East San Diego. When we got there, it was closed, so we decided to walk to the house of her home girl Myesha who lived a couple streets down on Marlbrough.

When we got halfway there, a car pulled up beside us, and a dude got out of the car and called Vershawn's name. I immediately recognized him, it was D Loc, the same dude I used to terrorize in the group home. He was with another person, and I recognized him as well. It was this dude they called Tasue who was also from West Coast 30s Crip Gang, like D Loc. I didn't think that they recognized me though, so I didn't say anything.

Vershawn and D Loc had a few words, and then he got back in the car and they left. I told Vershawn about what went on between me and him in the group home. When we started walking down a side street, I saw the car that D Loc was in hit the corner. They stopped in the middle of the street, and D Loc got out and started walking towards us. Vershawn immediately started running, I stood my ground. I saw that he had a gun in his hand. I couldn't move, I was frozen in my spot. When he got around seven yards from me, he begin raising the gun, but then all of a sudden he turned and ran back to his car.

I didn't understand what had happened. I thought I was going to be killed or at least shot. When I turned around to see what had made him change his mind about shooting me, it became clear why. There was a police car parked in front of the apartments right behind me. God was with me that day.

I have had a lot of trauma and drama in my life. I've been shot, shot at, and I've been jumped by two different gangs on separate occasions but on the same day. Both gangs were Blood gangs, supposedly allies.

I have even been shot at by females. It's kind of funny, dangerous though, because someone could of gotten hit and seriously hurt. Me and the homie Frank Nitti was up at the four corners of death (Imperial Street and Euclid Avenue) at the Shell gas station, when some females pulled up in a blue Cadillac. We approached them and asked them what were their names. Basically they told us to go fuck ourselves.

Nitti went off and started calling them crab ass bitches (derogatory word for Crip) and they can fuck themselves back. Well, when they were finished getting their gas, they pulled off towards the exit. When they got there, one of the females stuck their hand out the car window and started shooting. We ran into the gas station market. They sped off through the light. That was crazy and unexpected.

The gang epidemic affected everyone; as you can see females got involved. Eleven year olds and some younger were involved. Gangs do not discriminate. Just like the bullet from a gangbanger's gun doesn't discriminate. The innocent suffers the most, because nine times out of ten, they are the ones who take the bullet intended for a gang member. Like Lotoya (I don't remember her last name), a beautiful girl who lost her life at a party in Spring Valley, California in 1996 from a bullet that was intended for someone else. So many senseless deaths, even when the bullets do find their mark, like in Bankster Reese's case. He was run over while riding his bike. It doesn't matter how many gangbangers one kills, it's not going to change a damn thing. You're not about to eradicate a whole gang off the face of this earth.

Yeah, they say that there will always be gangs. That maybe so, but we can change the gang's agenda. Like Tupac said "Love your hood but recognize that it is all good." It doesn't matter if you're Blood or Crip, the shit leads to a deadend. This was not the purpose for the original Crip movement. Black on Black crime; there's no Black Power in that. We all have war stories, but our "WAR" should no longer be amongst ourselves. The self hate has to stop. But we can't do it alone. It takes all of us. So, can we get some help?

Thank you for lending me your ears and eyes. I hope to work with all of you soon, so we can save the next generation from this genocide.

War Story

Depicted in depth, the murder of a
rival is just causal conversation
when it comes to gang affiliation.
We feel no remorse because
we label it as revenge.
We pour out some liquor
and get ready to kill all over again.
It's the life of a gang member
feared and hated, but I am a hero
to my gang, so death row doesn't faze me.
Ten years have passed and I heard
my homies stopped banging,
and every time I get a letter
I hear that shit is constantly changing.
The gang was my sanctuary,
my one and only glory as I sit on
death row telling my war stories.
Dead man walking is what I often hear,
which will be me one day being
escorted down the tier.
As I envision this process,
all kinds of thoughts go through my head,
but the one that hurts the most
is will I be missed when I am dead?

Chapter 17

Colors

The movie "Colors" was a complete disappointment to the Blood and Crip gangs. It depicted more of the Mexican gangs. But the hype of the movie caused a lot of drama all over the State of California. Up in the city of Sacramento, two young Blood gang members from the Athens Park Blood Gang in Los Angeles went to watch it. When they left the movie, they ran into a group from one of the Crip gangs in Sacramento. Guns were pulled and when the shooting was over, one of the Crips was lying dead. I was in New Folsom State Prison when it happened. One day in the dayroom, we overheard this Crip say that the guy who got killed was his little brother.

A year later, I was transferred to Pelican Bay State Prison. I then ran into the two young Athens Park Blood Gang members who now had been convicted of this murder. Two was representing red, while the other represented blue. Two ended up with life sentences, while the other one lost his life.

Donovan Simmons and Terry Moses

We all were very proud of the colors we represented. Little did we know that the color red or the color blue had become a deadly poison. And if you would have asked some of the sixteen to eighteen years olds at that time in 1988, how did the colors come into play with the Bloods and Crips, they couldn't tell you. Or some would come up with some new war version of what some one close to their age told them.

When the Crips hit the streets back in the late 1960s, you could not tell the difference from one gang from another, because we all wore the same kind of clothing. It was in 1973, when the color factor became so important in this drama. YTS stands for Youth Training School, which is also apart of the California Youth Authority. Gangbanging was really spreading at this time, some affiliated themselves because they thought gangbanging was where it was at. Some joined for protection, but one thing was for sure by 1973, it were a hell of a lot of black gangs fighting against each other.

YTS, as mentioned, is where most of us real troublemakers ended up at all at the same time. When you arrived, you were given a bandana, also known as a handerchief. This place was full of the most well known gang members in the cities of Los Angeles and San Diego. The Crips all started wearing the blue bandanas, while the Bloods started to wear the red ones. Those were the only two colors that were passed out.

This gang fad went to the streets from the California Youth Authority in 1973, and it's been represented that way every since. This gang color fad went from bandana to every other piece of clothing. The tennis shoe Chuck Taylor, also known as Allstars, made by Converse, were the most popular tennis shoe out at the time. Now, at first they sold the shoe only in white, black, and white and blue. By this time, no gang member that wasn't a Crip would be caught dead in anything with the color blue. I don't know if Converse caught on, but in 1975 they came out with a pair of red and white Chuck Taylors, known also as Allstars.

This is how we started to put tags on ourselves to our so-called enemies and to the cops. I mean everybody walked around sporting colors with an invitation to kill them. The shoestrings were the last thing to get popular. The Bloods wore the fat lace red shoestrings with anything they had on, while the Crips sported the blue ones. It got so popular that little kids started doing it even in elementary school. This was the most dangerous, stupid, and ignorant thing that was implemented into the gang lifestyle, because for one, you're making yourself the biggest target on the streets at a time when killing a rival gang member was better than having sex to the most hard core. Secondly, we were already young criminals, and we would do a crime any place or at any time, but were most likely caught because we were sporting the most noticeable colors that a criminal should not be wearing at all.

It got so bad that the Crips would no longer say a word with the first letter beginning with a B. For instance, if the word was Bay Bay, the Crips would say *Say Say*. The Bloods were the same. If a word started or had a C in it, they use the letter B instead. Like, for instance, Cigarette, the Bloods will say *Bigarette*.

A guy I know name H.B. was the best I ever heard with the gang affiliation slang. He could speak it in almost ever word he used. Like *bick back* and *be bool*, which in regular language he would say kick back and be cool. This shit was so serious, or *berious* as H.B. would say, the older people had no idea what these younger people were talking about.

I witnessed a lawyer look at a guy I know like he was speaking something totally foreign to him. The lawyer informed him that he had a new charge because the person he had robbed had just died. The young gangbanger responded by saying, "Blood, I'm berious and that's on everything I love. I didn't do it." The man looked at him and told hem to calm down and repeat that again but slowly, please.

There was so many killings behind someone wearing red or blue that it sounds sickening now to reiterate it through my memory. The one that is still fresh on my mind happened in the beginning of 1997. A high school girl was riding the bus home from school one day. She was a cheerleader, and the school color was red. The bus she was on stopped at a bus stop where a lot of Crips hung out at. The girl on that bus was spotted with her red cheerleader uniform on and was gunned down on the bus. She was not gang affiliated at all. She was, in fact, said to be one of the best students on campus.

It hit me real hard because I have a niece named Otika Horn who went to the same school and was also a cheerleader, and I used to always see her come home from school in her uniform. I mean you just don't know how you will respond to something like that until happens to your family. How can you even say "Rest in peace" when someone loses their life for something as senseless as that?

Can you even imagine how this girl's mother and father must feel, even today, ten years later? To think about their beautiful daughter losing her life because she was wearing her cheerleader's uniform home from school, and it just happen to be red. There's no sadder feeling than this. The senselessness of this act is beyond measure, because if you were to put it on a scale it would weigh nothing.

That is what the "now" gangbangers need to understand, that there is nothing to gain from gangbanging. Whether you represent the red or blue, your reward will be nothing.

Chapter 18

Just Call Me Joe

My first memories of violence were in the year 1965. The Crips and Bloods did not exist during this time. I was a very young boy at the age of seven but I remember vividly the hardship, discrimination, and racism that black people were going through. The Watts riot of 1965 resulted in the city being almost completely burned down. This was the first time I witnessed how violence affected people's lives. I was a kid but I understood that black people were fighting for equal rights and the opportunity to be able to feed their families without having to commit a crime.

Right after the Watts riots, the Black Panther Party was formed and the US Organization. These groups' goals were to educate, unify, and teach black people how to fight back economically and politically. These groups were looked upon like terrorist groups by the U.S. Government. So, by the time I was a teen, the black power movement had died and was being replaced by street gangs that would change a lot of lives forever in the city of Los Angeles, which is where I grew up.

With this new gang thing getting popular, a lot of the teens my age became products of our environment. During this period, the Los Angeles police and sheriff's departments that patrolled Watts, Compton, and all of south central Los Angeles did nothing but instigate gang warfare between the Bloods and Crips. They would literally bring a Blood into our neighborhood and announce "There is a Blood in your hood." And they would do the exact same thing to a Crip gang member.

I am revealing what I know, not something I heard. My gang neighborhood was the Back Street Crip Gang, and I was there one day when the LAPD pulled up on us and told us point blank that "the Blood gang is going to come through your hood and kill somebody, so what are you guys going to do about it?"

This went on in every neighborhood, but the gangs had started to put so much fear in the people with this terror and violence that to speak on this would have been totally unbelievable to the general public. This senseless violence is as fresh to me now as it was some thirty years ago, because nothing has changed. In fact, it has gotten worse. To make things even more tragic is the fact that a lot of the kids today that are losing their lives are not even gang affiliated.

I personally started gangbanging when I was twelve years old. My reason for joining the gang was because I had seen so much violence, and personally I had been abused as a child. So, by the time I became a teenager, I was ready to rebel at the first opportunity, because the gang gave me power and security in the sense that I would never be abused again. But in reality all the gang did was turn me into an abuser. Once. I armed myself with gang affiliation I became a complete juvenile deliquent.

I was in and out of Juvenile Hall so much that one time the judge sentenced me to a boys group home. The home was located in Compton, California. That is where I met

Crip co-founder, the notorious Stanley "Tookie" Williams. He was in full charge of the boys home at the age of twenty, which was in the year 1975. We all looked up to "Tookie" because he was one of the originators of the Crip gang. The police even feared "Tookie", and most of us wanted to be just like him. Stanley "Tookie" Williams was so strongly influential in my life that when he received the death penalty for murder I wanted to be on death row, too.

I speak the truth to show people that gang life consumed me like it was a drug. We had a phrase we used to use that said Crip or die, or Crips don't die they multiply.

It's been over thirty years since I was a teenager, but I am still trying to recover from that lifestyle. Sometimes I catch myself still dressing like a gang member and using that language as well. Personally I believe I still have a long way to go to recover from a lifestyle that dominated and had me believing that another black man was my true enemy.

One of the most inspirational moments in my life is when I heard that "Tookie" Williams was nominated for the Nobel Peace Prize. He denounced gangs and started having books published to guide the youth in a positive direction. It has inspired me deeply and my concept now is if "Tookie" could do it from a cell on death row, then damn it, so can I.

I would also like to take this opportunity to thank author Terry Moses for giving me a voice in this project. I'm not looking for a Nobel Peace Prize, just peace for our troubled youth of today. And if I can inspire and enlighten and be apart of the solution, then I feel strongly compelled to do so. I have nephews that I am sad to say are going down that same path, and if the original survivors don't stand up now, we will lose another generation of kids to this senseless cycle of madness. It is a generation headed for genocide, and I feel obligated to help bring this genocide to an end.

This is what author Terry Moses and co-author Donovan Simmons were trying to get us to understand that what we did in the beginning is being passed on with nothing but a fatal ending to look back on. Like the others who have given their testimony to a new beginning, I pray to God for forgiveness from my entire family and the African American community, and for the constant worry I caused my mother to suffer. I have seen first hand what loving parents go through when they lose their kids to senseless acts of gang violence. Far too many kids are being cheated out of life, like, the young girl by the name of Myesha that was killed while having dinner with her family in San Bernadino, California in 2005 and in Santa Monica, a young teenager walking home from school got gunned down for no apparent reason. He was one of the stars on the high school football team.

Also, a former LAPD chief lost his very own granddaughter in Los Angeles. She was gunned down while waiting in a drive-thru at Popeye's Chicken in the year 2000. Tragic also was the killing of a young lady by the name of Amber who sang at the police chief's granddaughter's funeral. Amber was killed while taking pictures with friends also in the year 2000. Tennis stars Serena and Venus Williams lost their older sister to gang violence. She was killed while sitting in a parked SUV in Compton, California.

My stepdad's great nephew was murdered by gang members in Los Angeles. He was thirteen years old and had begged the gunmen not to kill him, to no avail. He was shot more than fifteen times. I lost one of my nephews name Jamel to gang violence in Las Vegas in 1992.

That is just a very small number of lives that ended much too soon. With all that said, I am now very eager and highly motivated to pick up where Stanley "Tookie" Williams left off in helping the teens to understand that they are headed in the wrong direction. And I personally challenge all ex-gang members to step up to help with a mass problem that whether you believe it or not, you help ignite the flame of this destruction. Now I ask you, do you have the heart to help put it out?

I would like to leave this final thought to inspire peace in all African American communities that have been infested with gang violence. Mr. Stanley "Tookie" Williams, was executed by the State of California by way of lethal injection, but in the final chapters of his life he became my hero again. But this time in a positive way, because he left us with a formula in his books to follow him as we did in violence, this time with harmony and peace. So, I strive now for a better way for our youth.

I also have great respect for authors Terry Moses and Donovan Simmons for having the heart to do a project like this, and I want to thank all the ex-gang members who participated in this book. God bless all of you and all that have the opportunity to read this book, because my hope is for it to help the disadvantaged youth and give the surviving original gang members the courage to join us in this battle.

RESPECTFULLY SPEAKING
"BIG JOE SPAND"

Because of You

The choices you make will dictate
your future and fate,
because you will not live your life
to its full potential if you don't apply yourself
and pay attention,
because the knowledge
that you neglect to achieve
will only allow you to be trapped in poverty
and so easily to be deceived,
because it is your fate that is created
by your own action,
making it vital that you pay attention
so that in your own life
you will not come up missing .
where you then will only exist and
the real fruits of life you can forget,
because the karma that you created
left you angry and uneducated,
resulting in you being poverty stricken
and drug addicted, filled with hatred,
and now you're blaming society
for your lack of education,
when it was you who decided
to send your own education
on a permanent vacation,
where I must again mention
because you failed to pay attention.

Chapter 19

Early Gang Devastation and Death

People for years have been misled and under the assumption that the gangs in the 1970s were fighting with their fists, chains, and knives. They were told that nobody was getting killed. So very far from the truth. The devastation of these gangs started when they first hit the streets full force in around 1971. As mentioned, the Hollywood Palladium gang killing of a guy over his leather jacket was the first that got everyone's attention.

I believe the reason for people being misled is due to these earlier gang killings not getting national or even sometimes local attention. In Watts, early 1973, we had two of our homegirls stop by this hole-in-the-wall fast food spot, which was located on One Hundred and Tenth Street and Compton Avenue. This place sits right next to the Nickerson Garden Projects, which is where the Bounty Hunter Gang started.

The homegirls were walking home from school when they decided to stop at the fast food spot. While waiting for their food, one of them had to use the restroom. So, she asked the man working at the counter if she could use the bathroom. He told her to go ahead. After a few minutes go by, the other female started to wonder what was taking her so long. The guy told her he'd go check and see.

When the man didn't come back right away, she decided to go check for herself. When she entered the restroom she saw her friend lying next to the toilet with her panties around her ankles and the man from the counter standing over her. She immediately ran back to the projects and told some Bounty Hunter Gang members that her friend was getting raped at the fast food spot.

Now, the projects have always been protective of their women, even before the Bounty Hunter Gang came out, so she got a immediate response. All they wanted to know was where was this fast food spot. They ran to the place with no intention of asking any questions. The homegirl's word was law.

When they got to the place, they immediately opened fire through the window. When all the shooting was over, the man at the counter lay dead with over thirty bullet holes in him. This took place in 1973. I was still in the California Youth Authority at the time of the shooting. My best friend, who not too long ago came to visit me, ended up getting a life sentence for the shooting.

There are hundreds of gangbangers doing life sentences for gang-related murders from the 1970s, even more from the eighties. But the difference is in the 1970s there wasn't much media attention. A lot of times these killings wouldn't even make it in the newspapers unless it was the Sentinel, which is a black-owned paper. You sure wouldn't see it on the five o'clock news. If it was black on black it wasn't newsworthy in the 1970s.

When the air was cleared, it was found out that the man at the counter didn't rape the homegirl. In fact he was just helping her off the floor after she had fell down. She had taken some barbituate pills, better known on the street at the time as red devils. The effects of these pills are very powerful; in fact, they used to have us walking around like we'd been drinking all day.

The bottom line is the man lost his life for nothing, and the only thing I want to show here is how serious this gang thing was from the time it started to this very present. When you hear the words gang war, that is just what it was.

In the year of 1972, at Jefferson High School, the results of this early devastation were evidence of how serious it was. Jefferson High was having its annual homecoming parade when the Crips got into a shootout with the then-called Eastside Ace Deuces. When the shooting commenced, the band was playing and the homecoming queen was waving at the crowd. She was one of the first people to get shot in the crossfire. One of the Crips who I knew named Koolaid was also shot. He took a bullet in the mouth that damaged his speaking ability for life. Others were injured as well, but not as severely as the ones mentioned. There were lots of incidents like these that were just forgotten about because at the time it was strictly an inner city problem, meaning the gang situation.

Now, if something like that happens it will be local and national news. The problem is bigger now that we all understand, but it's the same result from the devastation now as it was in 1971 or 1972. Killing is killing, no matter what era it happens in. The point here is not to compare the eras of destruction, but to shed some light on some of the history and the people who have been forgotten, because as tragic as these events were they did not get any media attention. So, these memories are only in the minds and thoughts of us who were there and have survived to be able to now share some of the most horrific events that took place and keep the memory alive of those who have been forgotten about who fell victim to this devastation.

I can't help but remember what happened at the funeral of Country. He was a well known gang member from the Original L.A. Brim Gang. He was gunned down by rival gang members but it didn't end there. At his funeral, a group of Crips rushed in the funeral home with guns, kicked over the casket, and begin shooting up the place. This was the first time anyone in the gang community ever heard of something like this happening. It definitely fueled the flames of hatred between the gangs. But it was an event that people never heard about. Why? I will say it again: because it was a inner city gang war, black on black, and to be truthful I believe no one cared but the people that it affected directly.

I remember when we lost our first homeboy to a gang killing. His name was George Henderson. He was killed at a party back in 1972. We were shocked and hurt and responded with rage. Even though we were hurt, the pain is still not like a mother losing her child. That is one of the worst sights you can ever witness. Just the sight of a mother mourning would send the other gang members into a revengeful state of madness.

After the malicious act that took place at Country's funeral, everybody from every gang started to go to funerals with guns. Some even hoped and prayed that it would happen like that again so they can release their frustrations of the loss of a comrad. That's just the way it was. It wasn't right, but every time someone was killed from one gang you could bet your last dollar that someone from the other gang would lose his life, too.

I lost one of my closest friends from childhood due to a gang-related killing. It was 1980, and I was still recovery from a PCP lab explosion where me and three of my friends were burned over seventy percent of our face and bodies.

Bloods and Crips The Genesis of a Genocide

This happened in 1979. So, 1980 started off real bad because we lost David Roy Lynch, another childhood friend in the explosion.

I started moving around better after six months of skin treatment and physical therapy. So, I was back hanging out with my folks again doing "our thing." That's what we called it back then. The night, my friend Rhea Boyce was killed. We were hanging out on One Hundred and Eleven Street. I was still wearing my burn suit under my clothing to keep the skin from rising while it was healing. It was Rhea, Ann, Scoope, Bird, Ray Harthorne, and Ronnie a.k.a A.D. We were drinking beers, and selling our PCP to customers as they walked by, when this guy came along with a pit bull dog.

Rhea asked the guy to come over and let him see his dog. Rhea was good with dogs. It seemed that he could make them do anything he wanted. He was rubbing the dog and asking questions, like did he fight his dog. The guy replied that he didn't. So, Rhea told him he had a nice dog and the guy said, "Thanks. I'll see you guys later." Before the guy could turn the corner he shouted "Look out!"

When we heard "Look out!" the car that he was warning us about was already upon us with guns sticking out of the windows. All we could do was duck, run, or just lay down on the ground, I did the latter. The shooting lasted around six or maybe seven seconds. Once the shooting was over, all you heard was people screaming out in pain. When I raised my head up the first thing I saw was that Rhea had been shot full blast in the face with what looked like a shotgun. His whole body was bucking off the ground because he was choking on his own blood.

All I could do was turn him over on his side so he would stop choking. While I was holding Rhea, I started to look around at the chaos from the aftermath of the shooting. All the people mentioned above had been hit by buckshots, except Ann and me. There was another guy laying dead who had just walked up to make a PCP purchase. He was shot in the back. It felt like everything was now moving in slow motion. People were hollering for someone to call a ambulance for the wounded.

I then heard somebody shouting my name "No, Terry, no." Rhea was still alive when the police and ambulance arrived, but barely. The first thing they did was try to make me get away from my friend, but I was not moving. So, they cuffed me up and placed me in the backseat of the police car. That was the last time I saw my friend alive. They pronounced Rhea dead while I was at the police station.

Rhea Boyce was one of the most feared guys from the Nickerson Garden Projects. He had the reputation of a knockout artist. He could knock a person out with either one of his hands. And coming from someone who knew him better than most, he did not like guns. He never used them or kept them around.

But he was killed because of one, due to the fact that it didn't matter who you were. When the gangs came to kill, that's usually what happened. The tragedy of Rhea's death took place in 1980, a very long time ago, but in my memory it repeats itself almost every single day and probably will for the rest of my life.

Chapter 20

Stand Up to Adversity

Facing adversity is not an easy task, especially when you were born and raised in the ghetto. It takes a very strong will not to give in to all the adverse activities that go on in any ghetto.

I personally did not face adversity well. I gave in and became a career criminal, but this is not just about me. My intention here is to share some truthful facts about quite a few people I know that stood tall in the face of adversity and were able to rise to personal great heights in their lives.

I have a childhood friend whom I grew up with and to this very day I still have the utmost love and respect for him. His name is Larry Gray. Our families were a part of the first original families that moved into the Nickerson Garden Projects in Watts, California when they opened back in the mid-1950s. So, me and Larry went to elementary school together.

They had a small family, two boys and two girls. Sister Gray was the older of the girls while Tanya was the baby of the family. Larry was the younger of the boys. William Gray was the oldest of them all. I never saw their father, which was normal for most of the families in the projects. Their mother was the force of the crew. We called her Ms. Del. She was one mean lady to us as kids. All that coming around at night time to get Larry to come out and play, it wasn't happening in that house. We respected Ms. Del so much that we stop trying to get Larry out when he was supposed to be doing his homework or cleaning the yard. She would not let Larry get off track from his education. And when I think about Ms. Del today, I admire her even more now, because I understand that she was helping her son to face adversity that would surely come his way.

By the time we made it to middle school, people were already looking at Larry like the next great basketball star to come out of the projects. When we were all fourteen years old, Larry had grown to be at least six feet four in height. We all played ball, but Larry took serious interest in playing and soon became the talk of the town.

During our first year in high school, the gang explosion invaded the streets of Los Angeles, and that's when everything changed. Jordan High School was the school we had to attend. But now the problem was if you were from the Nickerson Garden Projects, your life was now in great danger. The reason being that the high school sits right next to the Jordan Downs Projects, which were now the J.D Crips and the Hickory Crips.

The Bounty Hunter Gang was their main rival from the Nickerson Garden Projects. My friend Larry Gray never gangbanged with us but was from the projects and to your rival, that meant you were one. The majority of the people who went to Jordan High that was from the Nickerson Gardens Projects changed schools, because like I said even if you didn't gangbang, you were labeled by where you lived.

Larry Gray stayed at Jordan High and went to school every single day. He went through hell but continued to show up. He lead the school to a championship season in basketball. He graduated with honors in light of the killings and fighting that were going on at the school between the gangs. Larry Gray went on to college at New Mexico State and Long Beach State, but he blew his knee out in his last year of college. That injury stopped him from being picked in the NBA draft. So, he went overseas and played professional ball there.

When he came back to the States, he started working with kids in the juvenile system. From there, he went to the Department of Corrections, and the last thing I heard about my friend was that he was a lieutenant on his way to being captain.

It's not easy growing up in the projects, but I want to express my deepest love and respect for someone who did, but stood tall in the face of adversity that came his way. And to his mother, Ms. Del, who we thought was so mean, she is now respected and admired by us all because she did what she had to do to make sure her son understood that if he didn't pay attention, he would fall prey to the self-destructive way of life that so many of us fell victim to.

Contrary to what most people used to think about neighborhoods that were polluted by gangs, there have always been more people in that hood that did not gangbang than did. And I believe now that if the other gangs and the police would have been taking this into consideration when they went to terrorize a neighborhood, so many innocent people would not be dead today.

I'm no exception to this terror. Because I can remember how we used to apply peer pressure to the guys who wanted nothing to do with the gangs. This is why I respect them so much today, because I know first hand what they had to go through living in a gang-infested area.

Donovan Simmons and Terry Moses

In the late 1960s, a family moved into the Nickerson Garden Projects that became known all over the world as the Sylvers singing group—James, Leon, Charmine, Edmond, Foster, and Olympia. They have two other girls but I never knew their names, because they were babies when they moved into the projects. James Sylvers was one of my childhood friends. We played sports together, and then hung out and chased girls together. They came into the projects with both of their parents, which was rare. They used to practice singing in their living room, and when there was a talent show they would be there. They had the big Afro's like the Jackson Five had, so from the start a lot of girls were always trying to be around them. They were a very close family. And they went through all the drama that any other family went through that lived in the projects.

But I remember vividly when the gangs exploded on the scene, none of the Sylvers boys or girls took part in them in any kind of way. This is vital because people in all projects have had to carry the bad reputation that came with living in those conditions, but the point is that they all were just concerned about their kids getting an education, eating, and staying alive long enough to make it out of the projects. And if that's not facing adversity then there's no such thing.

It is a well known fact and on public record that the following celebrities were once gang-affiliated but changed their lives and were able to rise to stardom. DJ Quick, one of the most successful rappers of all time, was once affiliated with the Tree Top Piru Blood Gang in Compton, California, and even as a star he caught hell from his peers. But he rose above all the nonsense and told the whole world (on his hit song "You A Gangster") That "he wasn't a gangster but a provider, and if it don't make dollars it don't make sense." Proud to be walking in his shoes now, instead of doing a life sentence somewhere or on death row or even worse, dead.

Adversity is something we, and I mean as black people, have always had to face. But we put up another obstacle in our own path, that obstacle being inner city gang warfare. We instituted harm instead of an education when we as the originators started these gangs. We took away black power and employed self-destructive tactics.

Now, almost forty years later and thousands dead, we need to step over all boundaries and try our best to give our youth something to live for other than the color of a rag. That is why at every opportunity we must show the troubled youth that these obstacles can be knocked down.

National Basketball Association star Andre Miller is a great example of a person being able to beat the odds of poverty and self-destruction in the ghetto. He grew up in Watts, California in Los Angeles during a time when a drug dealer and gangbanger was the most popular choice for most teens. I grew up with most of his uncles and aunts in the Nickerson Garden Projects. He grew up around hardcore gangs and drug dealers. But he never fell victim to the peer pressure that everyone who lived in the neighborhood faced. He watched some of his childhood friends self-destruct to both, gangs and drugs.

He attended high school right next to the projects called Ver Bendel High. From there he went to Utah University and led his team to a national championship game. He is now an NBA star whom everybody in Watts should be damn proud of. He let it truly be known that a person can do anything, no matter what type of environment you were brought up in. Every time I see him play, it gives me great pleasure to say he's from the neighborhood.

There are countless people that grew up in gang-riddled neighborhoods but did not participate. But their lives were in just as much danger, because when a rival gang came shooting they were not asking the question, "Are you from the gang?" The entire neighborhood was the target. This is the most forgotten thing about the madness of gang warfare. The innocent usually are the ones to suffer, and even worse was the fact that people could not just up and move because if that were the case they wouldn't be living in the projects or in a low income district.

The effect that the gangs had on the entire city of Los Angeles was enormous, but let us not forget people like R&B singer Tyreece. He grew up in Watts when bullets were flying on the way to school and after. But he did not fall victim to the peer pressure. He is a major success story from straight out of the ghetto. And believe me if you went to Markham Jr. High or Jordan High School, both in Watts, and you didn't gangbang, you caught hell from every gang. I mean, from getting chased home, shot at, or even worse, stabbed or killed.

From the Coca Cola commercial singing on the bus that we all remember to the Grammies and big screen, Tyreece had done it all, and times were just as hard for him and his family as it was for everyone living in Watts. But he showed us, just like Andre Miller did, that you can pull through in hard times if you believe in yourself and keep your eyes on the prize. For me personally, that's what the term "Watts Up" is really about standing up to adversity even though the odds are against you. And they will surely tell the world that if they could do it, then so could the next person.

You know a few years back we lost one of our greatest motivational stories ever. The beautiful Florence Griffen Joyner, better known to the world as Flo Jo. She too grew up in Watts dodging bullets from gang warfare. She went on to become the world's fastest woman and set several records at the 1988 Olympics. She even made a fashion statement every time she stepped out on the racetrack. She showed the world that it was okay to be beautiful, talented, and tough. She was truly one of the greatest inspirational stories to come out of the town we call Watts. And she will always be loved and remembered with the utmost respect.

Chapter 21

Lost Love

This one is for all the Southeast females who once represented the red or blue flag. We speak so much about the men affected with this vicious disease that we overlook the women who have been plagued with this sickness. It's time to shed a light on this growing epidemic. The thing about a female gang member is, usually in most cases, they start representing a gang because of their man. If their man is from a gang, nine out of ten times, they're going to start representing his gang. This is were the term "hood hoppers" comes from. They jump from one gang to the next because they break up with one dude from a certain gang, and then they start messing with someone else from another gang and start claiming his neighborhood.

But not all females are like that. You have some who stay true to their gang no matter who they're with. Not only do they stay down for their "hood," they represent it to the fullest. They'll fight, stab, and kill for their neighborhood. You know the saying "Can't stop, won't stop."

This is not to glorify or dignify; I'm just telling it like it is. I have seen first hand the extremes a female will go for her set. I have witnessed my homegirls Toya and Rochell (from Skyline Eastside Piru Blood Gang) take on six females at once. And they were the instigators. I have seen Rocquell (from Lincoln Park Blood gang) knock a dude smooth out. I had a homegirl named Racey Rachell (R.I.P.) who single-handedly terrorized Downtown San Diego. She even shot one of the homeboys. I've been with 17 homegirls (from Skyline and Opharrel Park Bankster Bloods) Toya, Deanna, Kelly, Kesha Bo, Angel, Donna, Jennifer, Brandy, Roshell, and Tanya, just to name a few, who were ready to put in work for their neighborhood.

I remember the time when we were in T.J (Tijuana) at a club called Club XS, when we got into it with some Lincoln Park and Emeralds Hills Bloods. It was like fourteen on eight. Eight being us, fourteen being them. And out of our eight, three of them were females, and they stayed down, fighting toe to toe with us.

There have been a lot of incidents involving females like the ones above. That's why it's not surprising that the fastest growing trend in the gang community is female gang-bangers. You'd be shocked to know the number of females who lost their lives and are serving life sentences due to their involvement with a gang. It's time for a wake-up call, because now it's affecting the mothers of our next generation. And if this epidemic is allowed to go on unchecked, then the kids of the future don't have a chance. It'll be "Gangs R US," and the new social norm of our society. We can't have that.

So, let's do everything in our power to detour off the path our black communities are headed on, which is self-destruction or better yet genocide. So, this one is for you: Tosha G, Deanna, Kandy, Robin Robinson a.k.a Ms. Skyline, Tinisha Bo, Tosha, Ebony, Key Key, Hollie Herrod, Holly Davis, Angela Bo, Ladie Red, Net Atkins, Nena Thompson, Ladie Soft, Cynthia Simmons, Latoya Hollands, Shinsha Washington, Myesha, Trish Bo, Renika Gay, Sonya Swanigan, Sonya Cruz, Chocolate, Ms. Deuce Five, Dahisha, Rosheda Ivory, Missy, Rocquell, Linda, Nykia, Pumpkin, Tonya Lee, Michelle Jones, Kim Parther, Tammy Banks, Doobie, Jennifer, Jennifer Ford a.k.a Vanilla, Teresa, Evon, Elizabeth, Laquesha, Brook, L.A. Fren, Monique, Alice, Joy, Porsha, Fatima, Nena Carter, Kesha Poole, Little Bit, Tracy Heard, A.O, Angel, Mrs. Green Eyes, Trelia, Killah Bo, Dee Dee, Desiree Holiday, Delacia, Kimmy, and Erika P. And for the ones I didn't mention, this message is for you, too.

If you already eradicated this cancer out of your life, then congratulations. I hope you continue on living a positive and a mentorous life. And I pray we can get your help in educating our sisters in the futility of gangbanging well until we cross paths.

Much love,
Nitti.

As we rapidly approach 2009, just as Nitti said, the fastest rate of increase in gang activity is teenage girls. And I now quote Lawyer Constance Rice, where she states the girls have gone from being sex objects for the male gang members to committing felony assault, and some are creating a power base of their own. Now, while this may be breaking news for the general public who has failed to pay attention to an epidemic that has now spread into the suburban streets, it is as old as the Crips and Blood gangs.

Female participation dates back all the way to the very beginning of the Crips in 1969. The very first popular female gangbanger was a girl that everybody called Crip Connie. It was said that she was the girlfriend of one of the founders of the Westside Crips, Stanley "Tookie" Williams, who was executed by lethal injection in 2005.

It was no big deal to see Crip Connie bailing down the street with two hundred Crips, and sometimes she would be right there in front of the pack. Every gang knew about Crip Connie back in the early days of these gangs' existence. From Crip Connie's female gang participation, the girl gang epidemic started to spread. And there was no other female whose name was known and respected as a gang member like Crip Connie.

After Crip Connie came Cynthia Nunn, the older sister of Marcus Nunn a.k.a China Dog. Cynthia became well known as a Compton Piru girl in the early seventies. Female gangbangers just got more and more popular as the war intensified into the mid-1970s. Girls wanted more power so they started forming their own offspring gangs like the Cripettes, the Bounty Hunterlettes, and the Pirulettes. (Please note: My intentions is not to glorify, only to share the facts as they occurred.)

In the mid-1970s you started to hear a lot of stories about female shootings and stabbings resulting from gang affiliation. In the year 1978, our entire girls drill team was attacked during the Watts Christmas parade. Some were Bounty Hunterlettes and some weren't. But they all represented the Nickerson Garden Projects, and that's all that mattered to our rivals. The parade started in Compton and ended in Watts, so the homegirls sporting their red and white outfits started doing their steps, when out of nowhere a crowd of Crip girls and guys attacked them.

After the fighting was broken up, they regrouped and continued on in the parade. As a tradition, everybody from the projects waited on our drill team to get to Central and Imperial, which is where the Nickerson Garden Projects starts. Now, we're all there waiting to cheer them on, with Staphaine Green out front, but as they came into view they were all mad with their hair all over their heads.

We all wanted to know what the full details of the attack, and we immediately went into action to defend our homegirls. None of them was badly injured, but as mentioned a lot of the girls were not even gang affiliated but attacked just the same.

In the year of 1981, our homegirl Gail Brown lost her life in a shooting that left two dead and another shot several times, but survived. Gail was with Jay and Big Rat, when they pulled into a gas station. While Gail was paying for the gas, Jay was in the car. Big Rat was at the back of the car pumping the gas, when several guys with guns jumped out of a van and opened fire on all three of them. When the shooting was over, Gail Brown lay dead not five feet from the car. Jay was dead inside of the car, and Big Rat was laying at the back of the car full of bullets, but still alive.

The point here is, that no matter if you were, female or male, once you became gang affiliated by association or participation, you become a target. My girlfriend at the time when the Bounty Hunter Gang came out was Sheila Matthews. She was a country girl from Arkansas that got involved with the gang through me. They carried our guns and were there when we needed them. But like I earlier stated, the females were starting to want some say so. They use to come to our gang meetings and try and dictate what we should or should not do.

I personally kicked them out of our meetings for good. Not long after that, Sheila started her own gang called the Gangsters. People around the neighborhood then tagged her with the name Sheila Gangster. Fortunately, Sheila pulled her life together. She became a devoted Christian and has lived that way for over thirty years now. Her best friend during those days was Cari Lewis. They were always together; every time you saw one, you saw the other.

Cari was the girlfriend of one of my childhood friends name Micheal Dorrough, an Original Bounty Hunter who is now serving a life sentence with no possibility of parole. Cari went on to be a Compton police officer for a few years. Then she went into social work where she has been now for over thirty years. I share this to say that not everybody involved with gangs ended tragically.

My homegirl Kathy Cavitt was not as fortunate as Sheila and Cari. Kathy had a boyfriend named Sam, who was a Crip. Kathy's whole family was associated with the Bounty Hunter Blood Gang. Kathy and Sam became so involved that they got married. So, now out of respect for the homegirl we allowed Sam into our neighborhood. They had a child together and seemed to be really in love.

One night they drove off to visit some people they knew outside the projects. When they arrived, the ladies started to gossip while the fellows went outside to have a smoke. Only problem with the smoke was, it was PCP, so, when they were through, they went back inside to kick it with the ladies.

Once inside, Sam pulled out a pistol and shot Kathy, his wife, in the head at point blank range. It killed her instantly.

He then turned the gun on another female and shot her and then he walked out of the house. He was caught a few hours later, still out of his mind from the PCP.

The moral of the story is the females who were gang members or associated with them have been suffering the same consequences as the males for a very long time. It is so obvious that the gangs of today get more attention now by the public and the media but the history of these gangs will show that females have been victims of this epidemic just like males have.

I believe that we must start being better role models for the youth of today whether they're male or female, because if we don't, the lyrics of a negative rap song will become a major player in the way that they think. We want to take this opportunity to dedicate this to all the females who have fallen victim to this nonsense past and present. Also, to the ones that have persevered, overcoming a way of life that offered nothing but teardrops and closed caskets.

We also want to make a very special dedication to all the mothers that lost a child to gang violence and again apologize for our participation as gang members. We can only look to the future now and do our best to end this cycle of madness.

Shattered Thoughts of a Black Queen

The life of a black queen is
hard in these trying times.
I lay awake after a night on the grind,
Committing numerous felonious crimes.
Bloody knife, bloody hands
Just because I didn't pay attention
And now my education
Went on a never-ending vacation.
Now the lack of education got me
Poverty stricken, priorities twisted
Gang affiliated hate just because of a location.
But as I sit on the block
With my gang rag in the correct pock,
Blood in, blood out
Is still what's it's all about.
My mom look at me like I'm a fool
Screaming "I won't stand for this mess
Unless you follow my rules."
She's not knowing though
My gang is the one who rules.
Bullets fly. Punctured lung, punctured wound
It's too soon someone whispers in the breeze,
But a body taken two shots

Now leaves someone else to grieve.
Tear drops, body bags, toe tags
As a little girl stares down at a body
While holding her mama's gang rag.
Her thought of revenge is evident.
This cycle will never end,
As she makes a vow to her mother,
"You'll soon see your killer once again."

Chapter 22

What If?

What if Raymond Washington, who was the co-founder of the Crip Gang, could have maintained the focus of what the word "Crip" originally stood for—Community, Revolutionary, Inner, Party, Services? It is also very important to understand that it's only a "what if" for people who knew what the true intentions of this group started out to be. It was an idea that got out of the control of the co-founders. The beneficiaries of these young blacks turning on each other were the Los Angeles police and sheriff's departments. I say this because what was going on in the City of Los Angeles at this time. Police brutality, racism, and poverty were the main focus of black people in the years 1968, 1969, and 1970.

One has to be able to conceive any kind of conspiracy theory in order to come close to being able to believe one. Black people in general were angry at the system, not one another. Some of the things that were going on should give you further insight.

There was a ruthless tragedy that took place in the year 1968 to a black man that is still fresh on my mind, and one of the most horrifying things I remember from my childhood. The incident took place on the Harbor Freeway in Los Angeles. The man was speeding on the freeway when he was stopped by the highway patrol. They signaled for him to pull over, but he kept on going. He stuck his head out of his window and waved for the highway patrol to come on.

They, for sure, thought they had a madman on their hands then. The chase went on until the black man decided he'd better pull over. When he did, he immediately jumped out of his car and started in the direction of the highway patrolmen, who were now standing ready with their pistols out. They ordered the man to stop and put his hands on his head, but he kept going towards them. He was not armed with any type of weapon, but when he didn't not stop, they shot him dead right there on the freeway.

When one of the highway patrolmen went to the car to secure the situation, he found a woman in the back seat of the car, having a baby. The man was trying to get his wife to the hospital because she was in great pain and the baby was coming out. The killing of this black man almost kicked off another riot in Los Angeles.

So, in search of what happened to our generation and what made us turn on each other, I said that to show that when this gang thing exploded into our lives, we were angry at the system, not each other. I believe that we became targets of a great big conspiracy. This theory is shared by more than just me, but the destruction caused by the Blood and Crip Gangs in the following years made this view unbelievable.

So, what if Raymond Washington's original concept would have stayed intact? I believe there would still have been a lot of lives lost. But the lives that were lost before the Bloods and Crips were more of a sacrifice for equal rights and overall better living conditions for suppressed blacks in America. It is a great big difference because these people before us will be remembered for trying to make a difference and a better way for their people.

Now, on the other hand, our generation lost its black pride and started to represent colors and street corners. We destroyed black power by killing each other and if the cycle of this madness doesn't stop, future generations of blacks will continue to be born into hatred for no more than the name of a street or color of a rag.

There is so much to be revealed that people just don't know. Like, when Stanley "Tookie" Williams was given authority to run boys' homes by the City of Los Angeles. And, as we all know, "Tookie" was one of the leaders of the original West Side Crips. The concept of putting "Tookie" in charge of these boys' homes was not to turn them into gang targets for rival gangs. The concept was to put someone in charge that could lead the youth in a positive direction. This started in 1971, but by 1972 if you were not affiliated with the Crips Gangs, these boys' homes became off-limits.

This one particular boys' home that "Tookie" was in charge of became a well known target, also. People would get shot all the time because the place was always getting shot up by the Piru Blood Gang. It was located in the city of Compton where the Compton Crips and Compton Piru gangs were already at war with each other. There were a lot of influential people that attempted to put this black-on-black gang explosion to a stop. Like, Ted Watkins of the W.L.C.A.C., which stands for Watts Labor Community Action Committee. Bob Collins, Gene Jackson, and the group known as the Sons of Watts.

This destructive way of life became too large for any of the above to handle. The gangs were so large by 1972 that we were now in the mind state that we ran the streets and nobody could tell us a damn thing. I remember when the Sons of Watts and Gene Jackson of the W.L.C.A.C. brought the gangs together for an attempt at a truce.

The Watts festival was coming up and, like I said, the gangs had gotten so big it would have been damn near impossible to stop a big breakout of violence between the gangs. The Watts festival was an annual event held at the then-named Will Rogers Park in Watts. It was a seven-day celebration of black pride. A parade was held on the seventh day. It was, at that time, the largest event held for black people in the City of Los Angeles. People came from all over to enjoy a full week of black entertainment at its best, and it would have been tragic if the gang situation was not under control.

So, the W.L.C.A.C. foreman called on the gangs to make peace with one another. A meeting was held to talk things out. The meeting took place at the school on One Hundred and Twelfth Street, which was in the Bounty Hunter Blood Gang territory. Some of the gangs that attended, besides the Bounty Hunters, were the Compton Piru Blood Gang, the East Side Crip Gang, the Carver Park Crip Gang, the Hickory Street Crips, and the Mona Park Crips. The entire school ground was just about filled with gang members.

We talked it out and came to the conclusion that we could get along and let the people enjoy themselves at the festival. At this meeting, there were at least five hundred gang members, and this was in 1972, when this was still young, so to speak. It was a week before the festival was supposed to start, so the gangs got together and partied together for the first time. This was a real attempt at peace. The Bounty Hunters invited the Craver Park Crips and some of the Compton Crips into the projects to our

Bloods and Crips The Genesis of a Genocide

weekly skating events followed by a dance. We got to know each other for the first time on a friendly level.

Once the Festival started, people were pretty much at ease because of the truce that had been made with the gangs. The problem was no one took the time to invite the West Side Crips to the truce meeting. So the very first night of the festival, all hell broke loose between the gangs. When the shit hit the fan, so to speak, people were getting shot or stabbed. The Los Angeles Police and Sheriffs were there with riot gear on, taking whoever they got their hands on and putting them on one of the two buses they had parked close by in case of something like this happening.

As mentioned, this took place in 1972, and that was the last time a gang truce was mentioned for twenty years. By me being there from the beginning of this madness, I can honestly say that we, the original gangbangers, destroyed a lot of the African cultural events in Los Angeles. Because to sponsor any event in L.A. was surely to attract the gangs, and that meant more than likely someone was going to lose his life.

So, what if "Tookie" Williams, who at this time was the most influential gang leader in the city, could have turned the gangs' focus back to black self-respect, pride, and black power? I strongly believe that if we wouldn't have been wasting so much of our energy and time on trying to kill one another, people like Sylvester Scott, a.k.a Puddin, who was one of the founders of the Piru gang, could have some day became a mayor of a city. I say this also of "Tookie" Williams, because so many people looked up to the both of them. I knew both of these guys, so I speak from what I know about them.

I say knew because "Tookie" Williams was executed by lethal injection by the State of California in November of 2005. While on death row, he wrote eight books, he denounced gangs, and he inspired the youth to get an education. Thousands or people tried to convince the governor that this was now a man that could do more good alive than dead. The people tried, to no avail; now I can only ask "What if?" to his situation.

We must always remember what happened to "Tookie" and let it be a wake-up call that it could happen to anyone who chooses this type of life. Sylvester "Puddin" Scott died in 2006 after being shot and paralyzed in the nineties. He was never really well again after being confined to a wheelchair. His following was enormous, and I can only imagine now what this guy could have accomplished and also inspired others to accomplish if, again, his focus had been geared in a more positive direction. As black people, we needed more strong leaders that people would listen to, because our leaders were getting killed by a different kind of gang. I say this because when I look back on those years I realize that black people were suffering enough by the system. We just added to our own hardship with the Bloods and Crips madness.

We witnessed the killing of a black man by the Los Angeles Police Department that was so brutal, black-on-black gangbanging should not have crossed any of our minds. In the year of 1970, a black man named Jerry Lee Amy had just returned from fighting for this country and was viciously gunned down.

The night he was killed, he was attempting to visit a girlfriend, when the LAPD pulled up on him. He was knocking at the door when they informed him that they had gotten a disturbing the peace call. He was then told to put his hands over his head but before that could happen, one of the officer shouted out "It looks like he has a gun." They then proceeded to empty their guns into Jerry's entire body. We were able to see this horrifying sight, thanks to the Black Panthers' newspaper. Some kind of way they had gotten a full naked shot of Jerry Lee Amy's body while he was lying dead on a flat bed. This was on the front page of the paper. There were bullet holes in his head, face, and even on the bottom of his feet.

So, I now ask myself how did we as young teenagers get turned against each other with all the hardship we were already facing and going through at that time? I strongly believe the answer is in the history of this destruction, which I think must be shared, viewed, and analyzed so it will never happen again.

My hope is for the younger generation to get a full understanding so they can vividly see that there is nothing waiting on them at the end of a life of gangbanging but a grave or a small cell on death row where they will suffer until they are executed. So, "what if" you just happen to take heed?

Epilogue

As we conclude, we wish to express our deepest apologies for our participation in something that was so devastating and non-productive in the African American communities. We also feel strongly concerned about some of the things that need to be done to stop this cycle of self-destructive madness. We believe we need a strategy to instill pride and hope into the inner-city youth to enable them to become responsible men instead of just another product of their environment. By saying that, we mean by not following in the same footsteps of the generation before them as drug dealers and gang members. We must provide a positive alternative to gang life now or we will lose another generation to this nonsense.

Homicide is the number one cause of death for black males from ages fifteen to twenty-four, and nationwide more than fifteen percent of African Americans drop out of school, and the teen rate for pregnancy amongst African Americans is still the highest in the country, which is one of the main reasons that thirty-three percent of African American children born in the United States are born into poverty.

These are the things that we know are facts about black teens. So, where does the healing start? Where does the hope begin? We believe it starts with the entire community. "Harambee" in Swahili means "let us work together."

We would now like to quote Dr. John M. Perkins: "I believe one of the surest ways to heal the inner city is by saving the boys of the inner city, because if we can reach the boys we can reach the entire community." That statement is so very important. As blacks in the inner city, a lot of us become fathers while we are still teenagers ourselves and the results of a young, uneducated black teen becoming a father is the making of a drug dealer or a gang member, which leads to a life of crime, which leads to an early death or a life sentence in prison.

Our youth need new heroes to look up to. They need to know and understand that if they struggle, but continue to strive and educate themselves that the sacrifice will enable them to make an honest living and not leave another African American child behind without a father, which is inevitable if they don't get an education. Because prison or an early grave is the only thing at the end of the tunnel for an uneducated African American man, which is also a factual statement.

By saving just one youth from a life of crime and gangs gives us the opportunity to save another one. As former juvenile delinquents, we can tell you that troubled kids want to be accepted as a part of something just like any other kid. But if the environment is poverty stricken, then gangs and drugs become the favorite choices. This is where the new heroes of these kids come into play. The ex-drug dealer, the ex-convict, the ex-gang member, these are the people that these kids understand and will pay attention to, but they have to see the success in the lives of these individuals. If you can display a certain amount of success from change, the struggle and hardship, then the message you are giving has conviction. The "each one, teach one" theory must come back into our lives as it once was during the Black Power and Black is Beautiful era. Harambee, "let us work together."

Everyone concerned will have to step up in the effort to save the inner city youth. There are celebrities in several states that have programs to keep these kids from falling victim to the harsh realities of the inner cities. Jim Brown, Maxine Waters, and Chaka Khan are just a few, but this is much bigger than any one millionaire. It is going to have to be the entire community that has to start raising these kids. A lot of them don't have mothers or fathers, and if they don't have concerned people in the community, then they have nothing in their eyes.

Donovan Simmons and I, Terry Moses, dedicated ourselves to this endeavor. I am now currently serving a life sentence in the State of California under the Three Strikes law. But from behind these walls we are reaching out to the Juvenile Halls, Boys and Girls Homes, and all other youth groups, sharing our stories with these kids to show them what's at the end of a life of crime and street gangs. And like previously said, if we can save just one it will give us the opportunity to save another one.

In regards to everyone that helped us or participated in this project, we thank you all profoundly.

APPENDIX

ROLL CALL

To illustrate the rapid spread of this Blood and Crip gang epidemic, I will list all the gangs by their names. Please note as you read this list that the Crips started in 1969, and Raymond Washington, formerly of the Avenues Street Gang, was the founder. The Crips started on the East Side of Los Angeles and is what the Original Crips went by, the East Side Crips. Every other Crip gang was an offspring of the original. Here is a list of all the Crip gangs from past to present that could be remembered: East Side, West Side, Main Street, Qute One 0 Two, Kitchen, One 0 Seven Block, Mafia, Hoover, Harlem, One Eleven, Neighborhood, Nine 0, Forties, Sixties, Eight Tray Gangster, Grape Street, Hickory Street, P.J. Watts, Compton Avenue, Carver Park, Carson Diloma Block, Sex Jerk, Avalon Four Tray, Five Deuce Broadway, Playboy Gangster, Compton Gandee, Swamp, Fronthood, Mona Park, West Boulevard, Santana Block, Eleven Eight East Coast, All the East Coasts, Pomona Ghost Town, Pomona Tray Five Seven, Gardena Shotgun, San Diego Neighborhood Forties, San Diego West Coast Thirties, Hot Gang, Lynwood, Long Beach Insane, Pasadena Raymond, Inglewood Raymond, Imperial Village, Lucky, Underground, School Yard, Water Gate, Nutty Block, Long

Beach Twenties, Altedena Block, Compton Tragnew, Syndicate, Payback, Franklin Square, One Twelve Neighborhood, Fresno 107 Hoover, Stockton North Side, Sacramento 29 Street, and the Six Deuce Diamonds.

These are most of the former and current Crip gangs from 1969 to 2008. The order of the gang names have no bearing on when they came out. This was done randomly.

As the Crip gangs grew, so did the Blood gangs. The L.A. Brim Gang was the only gang that was functioning as a street gang when the Crips arrived. The Crips' rapid spread of inner city terror made more Bloods emerge to fight against them.

This is a list of most of the Blood gangs past and present that could be remembered. The following are all Brims: Five Nine, Six Deuce, Black P Stone, Fruit Town, City Stone and the VNG. You have the Blood Gangs: The Bounty Hunters, San Diego Skyline East Side Piru, Miller Gangster, Compton West Side Piru, Fruit Town, 151. Village Town, Holly Hood, Centerview, Cedar Block, Tree Top, Lime Hood, 135, Elm Street, Mob, Capanala Park, Cabbage Patch, Hoover Family, Crenshaw Mafia, Pomona Four Five Six, Cross Altantic, Hicieinda Village, Family Swans, East Side Ace Deuces, Nine Deuce Bishops, Peblos Bishops, Circle City, Scotts Dale, Neighborhood Twenties, Inglewood Family, Queen Street, Neighborhood Piru, Pasadena Lanes, L.A. Lanes, Athens Park, Two Ps and a B, San Diego Five Nine Brims, San Diego Lincoln Park, San Diego Emerald Hills, San Diego O'pnarrol Park Bankster, San Diego Little Afrika Piru, Blood Stone Villains, Inland Empire Bloods, Oak Park, Louis Park Piru, Del Paso Heights, Frenso Swans, and the Bedrock Pirus.

It must also be stated that this list was not composed to glorify these gangs' existence, but to show how the genesis of this destruction spread into a form of self-inflicted genocide, This list includes well over a hundred different Blood and Crip gangs in the State of California, but these gangs are now in several different states, like Arkansas, Washington, and Arizona.

This senseless way of life has became like a disease that is resistant to antibiotics. I personally believe that the only way we can even come close to starting a healing process is for former gang members to step up and start educating the uneducated affiliated. And then we can start to let them know that they are fighting for nothing, and nothing is what they will get from the gang, oh, except an early death.

The Spirit And Legacy Of Tupac

Dear Pac,
Just to let you know that
you haven't been forgotten,
your lyrics of reality is still on and poppin,
you are being imitated and falsely duplicated,
but nothing has come close to the effect
that "Dear Mama" has had on us yet.
Your lyrics and legacy will forever live on,
but damn, nigga, we wish you weren't gone.
They're still living and dying in L.A.
and you can hear a Tupac song
every mutha fuckin' day.
There's not a metaphor or rapper
that could ever take your place,
and the world is still paralyzed
by the shit that you had to say.
Oh, yeah, and just the other day
a conversation occurred about the
greatest rap album from yesterday to today,
"All Eyes On Me" topped everybody's list
with nothing more left to say,
"Hell Mary young nigga" because
you were the most prolific and influential
rapper that this world has ever seen,

passionately real and lyricaly mean,
your ghetto knowledge will never be forgotten,
and since you made it to see God first
you can hit him up and tell him
that shit in the ghetto definitely got worse.

Introducing Calvin Offerral

We are honored now to introduce ex-gang member Calvin Offerral. Calvin is a born again Christian who inspires people to change their lives through his testimony of his personal battles with redemption. He has a book coming to bookstore next year, to be entitled "His Vision." Concerned with the Blood and Crip gang epidemic, he reveals in his book his vision of God's plan for these gangs.

B.	L.	O.	O.	D.	S		C.	R.	I.	P.	S
E	I	F	F	E	A		H	I	N	E	A
L	V	F		L	L		R	D		A	L
I	I			I	V		I	I		C	V
E	N			V	A		S	N		E	A
V	G			E	T		T	G			T
E				R	I		I				I
R				A	O		A				0
S				N	N		N				N
				C			S				
				E							

His Vision
By Calvin Offerral
Due out in 2009

Printed in Great Britain
by Amazon